SIGNIFICANT ISSUES SERIES
Volume I, No. 5

IMPLICATIONS OF SOVIET AND CUBAN ACTIVITIES IN AFRICA FOR U.S. POLICY

by

Michael A. Samuels
Chester A. Crocker
Roger W. Fontaine
Dimitri K. Simes
Robert E. Henderson

Copyright 1979

by

The Center for Strategic and International Studies

Georgetown University

All Rights Reserved

Library of Congress Catalog Number: 79-90797

ISBN: 0-89206-010-7

Introduction

T HE TRADITIONAL AFRICAN POLICY of the U.S. government has reflected the view that events in Africa were of interest, but not of high priority. Since the decision by the Portuguese government to give independence to its African colonies, there has been a significant increase in Soviet and Cuban activities in Africa. This increase has been most seen in Angola and Ethiopia. It has almost been as if the Soviets and Cubans had acted both with an understanding of the relatively low priority of Africa in U.S. policy and with the belief that post–Vietnam attitudes in the United States militated against involvement in areas of international tension.

This situation has led to a series of short–term crises of policy. There is increased concern within the U.S. government and on the part of outside observers about the appropriateness of U.S. policy and actions. Furthermore, several countries in Africa and many friends and allies of the United States in the Northwest quadrant of the Indian Ocean region and throughout the world are clearly worried. Many have voiced concern at the apparent lack of will of the United States to cope with Soviet and Cuban actions in the area and their broader ramifications; some have expressed fear that major Soviet activities in Africa may herald a change in the atmosphere of détente so serious that the prospects for congressional approval of a new Strategic Arms Limitation Treaty (SALT) agreement could be undermined, thus calling into question the fragility of presidential power in foreign policy.

We now find ourselves at a plateau where it is important to reassess the U.S. stance both toward Africa and toward the Soviets and Cubans in the context of their activities in Africa. Such a reassessment requires an understanding of three groups of factors:

1. factors in African politics that have created the opportunities for Soviet and Cuban activities;
2. the domestic and international factors in Soviet policy that have contributed to the changed activities; and
3. the domestic and international factors in Cuban policy that have contributed to the changed activities.

Such a rethinking is absolutely necessary as an element in devising an appropriate African policy. A major goal of such a

reassessment is to lessen the apparently reflexive and defensive character of U.S. policies.

The purpose of this paper is to assess the specific factors that have led to the geopolitical challenge presented by the Soviet Union and its Cuban allies. In so doing, a number of factors of vital concern to Africa, including economic development, human rights, and humanitarian concerns, have not been addressed as fully as they deserve. Some would argue that Africa should be viewed by Washington on its own merits without reference to the behavior of other outside powers. In the real world, this is impossible. Africanists must realize that there is a continuing competition for power between the United States and the Soviet Union; similarly, Soviet and strategic policy analysts would be short–sighted to ignore the interests, desires, and uniqueness of the African scene.

This paper analyzes the major components of the problem and suggests a number of concepts and actions for U.S. policy. An earlier version of this paper was used to stimulate reaction at a seminar of experts on April 20-21, 1979. A list of participating panelists is included in the appendix. Their frank and helpful comments and criticisms were important in revisions that have led to this final product. Only the authors, however, and not any of the participants, bear any responsibility for the views contained here. Similarly, although both the research and the seminar that have produced this study were funded by the Defense Department, the views, opinions, and findings contained in this report are those of the authors and should not be construed as an official Defense Department position, policy, or decision, unless so designated by other official documentation.

Many members of the Center for Strategic and International Studies staff provided invaluable assistance. Several deserve specific mention, namely Arvilla Brown, Jerry Sheehan, Steve Haykin, Rick Ehrenreich, Lyn Bickel, Wendy Price, Mary Ellen Iskendrian, Dale Gavlak, and Connie Lawson. Without their behind–the–scenes work, the seminar that critiqued the earlier draft could not have been successful.

Contents

EXECUTIVE SUMMARY
IMPLICATIONS OF SOVIET AND CUBAN ACTIVITIES IN AFRICA FOR U.S. POLICY

by

Michael A. Samuels
Chester A. Crocker
Roger W. Fontaine
Dimitri K. Simes
Robert E. Henderson

A reassessment of United States policy both toward Africa and toward Soviets and Cubans in the context of their activities, has led to a series of conclusions and recommendations for United States policy that can be summarized as follows:

1. It is legitimate and necessary to focus on the Soviet–Cuban dimension of African problems because of the importance of the relationship of the United States with Moscow and Moscow's often important role in African trouble spots. This focus should not be the only thrust of African policy, but it is a valid thrust and should not be down–played.

2. The growing Soviet and Cuban political and military involvement in Africa presents a serious challenge to U.S. interests. Nevertheless, not all activities of Moscow and Havana there are counter to U.S. interests. The United States cannot deter the Soviets and Cubans by pursuing exclusively defensive, reactive, and anti–Soviet policies. While sometimes such policies may be necessary as short–run responses, in the long–term perspective, concern about both Africa and Soviet advances recommends positive actions and policies.

3. Resources supporting a policy are key to its effectiveness. The United States should increase the resources it directs toward Africa commensurate with the importance of the continent and its increasing global significance.
4. Change in Africa is inevitable, and change itself is not necessarily inimical to U.S. or African interests. What matters is not the fact of change but how change occurs, whose interests and influence it reflects, and the extent of violent or coercive solutions.
5. Africa is a confusing and complex policy environment for Western policy. The prevalence of highly dependent and vulnerable states accounts for the growing number of African requests for outside support. Institutions in many African states tend to be fragile, and it is easier to damage them than to build them. Small increments of money and armed force make a big difference.
6. The facts of power and dependence in Africa have changed significantly since 1974 because of the growing number of conflicts, the growing infusion of arms, and the asymmetry in U.S.–Soviet attitudes toward involvement. Africa's regional system is in transition. The influence of Africans themselves will be reduced further if armed violence is the arbiter of current and future change. Given constraints on U.S. policy, Western influence will also suffer if diplomatic solutions fail.
7. The United States should develop policies to help construct viable political and security institutions in African countries. These would include support for more competent civil administration, political party structures, civilian police structures, labor union officials, and military forces. A successful policy cannot simply finesse the security dimension of African problems. Above all, bilateral relations and the needs and interests of individual states should be primary.
8. The biggest opportunities for a Soviet and Cuban presence in Africa will be the existence of white, minority–ruled governments. As long as such governments exist and follow discriminatory policies, the United States will be at a comparative disadvantage. In terms of relations with the vast majority of African na-

tions, an association with Pretoria is a liability even if it may be justified for other reasons. The United States should follow an active policy encouraging meaningful changes in minority–ruled states. U.S. diplomacy has a delicate task: on the one hand, to disassociate Washington from racist practices in Africa; and, on the other, to discourage the inclination to seek solutions through force and sanctions.

9. To eschew dealings with important political actors in Africa, such as Mozambique and Angola, because of presumed hostility toward the United States may be short-sighted. Even African states that profess Marxism–Leninism may have certain local foreign policy and security needs compatible with U.S. interests. Furthermore, the United States could pursue a "denial strategy" toward some important Soviet interests. A willingness to pursue an independent line free from Soviet or Cuban influence is an important criterion in determining U.S. policy toward the African left–leaning states connected with Moscow and Havana.

10. The United States should maintain closer collaboration and joint effort with other Western countries, for many of whom an active role in Africa is of even greater importance than for the United States. Western nations individually and jointly should not be deterred from taking initiatives that appear needed and promising because of potential charges of "ganging up" on Africa. There may be fields where joint Western initiatives could be more promising than efforts in global fora like the United Nations Conference on Trade and Development, the World Bank, etc.

11. Although some economic assistance should continue to be concerned with basic human needs and the rural and urban poor, there must be a closer coordination between political interests and economic support. The misnamed "security supporting assistance" program should be expanded and renamed to reflect its purpose as politically motivated assistance.

12. It is unlikely that the Organization of African Unity (OAU) and African peace–keeping capabilities generally will grow any stronger by themselves in the years ahead.

The United States should encourage regional security responsibility in Africa and assist certain African countries willing and able to provide such a capability. The eventual development of an African peace–keeping force under the auspices of the OAU should be encouraged.

13. As Africa is part of the non–communist world economic system, a better positioning of Africa in that system will benefit the West. The worsening economic conditions for Africa will provide fertile ground for Soviet propaganda and advances.

14. Bilateral agreements with the Soviet Union on Limitations on Conventional Arms Transfers and Naval Limits in the Indian Ocean may make long–range sense. In the short run, however, such discussions require an active policy of arms transfers and an expanded presence in the Indian Ocean. Signs of Soviet military restraint in Africa are a prerequisite for the trust necessary before the above agreements could be satisfactorily concluded.

15. A relatively high level of policy commitment to Africa is not sustainable unless it is based on public understanding and support. Without this commitment, the United States must be wary of overselling — there must be greater congruity between U.S. promise and performance in Africa. Therefore, the combination of domestic apathy and polarized emotions on African issues must be addressed. We cannot expect the Soviet Union to defer possible gains because we are unwilling or unable to act as if we believe that Africa is important.

16. Finally, the United States should take into account the fact that Soviet and Cuban activities in Africa represent an integral component of the overall foreign policies of these powers. Accordingly, in addition to anticipatory and reactive activities in Africa, the United States has to use leverages available in the framework of bilateral relationships, including both incentives and penalties. It is imperative to communicate to the USSR well in advance what kind of Soviet global role the United States is willing to accept and what elements of Soviet behavior in

Africa and other areas of international instability are considered particularly objectionable.

The above summary has resulted from a study for the Department of Defense by the Center for Strategic and International Studies.

Copies of the full study are available by writing:

> Publications
> Attention: Kenneth Small
> CSIS
> 1800 K Street, N.W., Suite 520
> Washington, D.C. 20006
> 202-833-8595

$4.00 per copy, 50¢ handling and postage.

I. THE AFRICAN POLITICAL SCENE*

Analysts of recent Soviet–Cuban behavior in Africa find it all too easy to polarize between two divergent views of the African climate. The first view holds that African nationalism, and the drive for nonalignment and racial dignity, are the best defense against communist ambitions. The second view stresses Africa's inability to resist the blandishments offered by Moscow and Havana. Each of these views can marshal recent events to justify its accuracy. Neither, however, is sufficient in itself.

Those who would buttress the first view show that Africans have resisted and will continue to resist external policies, both communist and anti–communist, aimed at reducing African independence by "using" Africa and Africans in cold war rivalries. Furthermore, adherents of the first view hold that Moscow and Havana can offer Africans only the instruments of repression, war, and liberation — not the instruments of development that African leaders have identified as their top priority. Moscow's abysmal record in providing economic and technical assistance offers a sharp contrast with the economic instruments, both public and private, available in the Organization for Economic Cooperation and Development (OECD) arsenal.

Some would take this analysis a step further and concede that the communist powers will obtain major influence during liberation struggles and during other forms of political transition, as in Ethiopia or, perhaps, Zaire. Since the Western powers are unable to compete in such endeavors, they are best advised to stand aside for the time being. Once stable government is re–established, the resulting African governments will inevitably be drawn into the Western economic orbit and weaned from their political dependence on the communist powers. Finally, such analysis points to the inherently unstable and "soft" quality of African politics. Regimes change quickly, and with them the often superficial ideological "stance" that is reflected in the foreign policy of many African states. The issues at stake in contemporary Africa have little to do with familiar Western dichotomies — democracy versus freedom; capitalism versus

---

* Principal contributors to this section were Chester Crocker and Michael Samuels.

communism — and much more to do with development, institutional modernization, and the emergence of an indigenously supported political order.

Set against this analysis is a second view that stresses Africa's vulnerability to the influence of and penetration by Moscow and Havana. This view argues that recent communist advances in Africa must be seen as an element of a longer historical process through which Western economic and political influence in Africa and other parts of the Third World have been undermined, Western will called into question, and the USSR's global power established. Evidence of the trend is seen in such central developments as the Soviet effort to outflank Western influence and interests in the geopolitically vital Red Sea–Persian Gulf arena.

Moscow's military support infrastructure has burgeoned over the past decade, especially in the more recent period since the Portuguese collapse and the Angolan civil war. In the process, the communist powers have established for themselves a position of primacy as Africa's leading security partner — as measured by arms transfers, training, base networks, troop presence — often at the expense of Western and Chinese influence. Accordingly, Africans who feel threatened, for whatever reason, or who wish to threaten other Africans increasingly will look to Moscow and Havana for support. Over time, it is argued, communist military and political assets will be sufficient to deter undesired forms of political change while promoting an accelerated and lasting reduction of Western credibility. Such expansionism has the further objective of weakening the economic and industrial fiber of the Western oceanic powers, which, unlike Moscow, are dependent on imported raw materials from within or around Africa. Resource denial, in sum, is seen as integral to this global expansionism that is by no means limited to Africa. Thus, a global pattern can be identified in which Africa will be a passive partner in a multi–continental and multi–oceanic strategy.

Taken together, these interpretations provide a statement of the problem confronting Washington. But each risks basic distortions by oversimplifying African regional order (and disorder) and African political aspirations at the state level of analysis. Neither view provides a basis for discriminating among various forms of Soviet–Cuban involvement or for iden-

tifying those scenarios most likely to damage Western interests. It is, therefore, essential to place current African developments and Soviet–Cuban opportunities in a broader political and historical context.

Elements of the African Regional Order

In historical terms, the current African regional order is young, and its bases incomplete. Boundaries drawn less than 100 years ago by Europeans provide only a skeletal basis for territorial security. Since they reflect the convenience of European statesmen in an earlier period, they bear little relationship to African demographic, economic, or political factors. Governmental institutions are similarly reflective of the colonial past. Though their staffing has largely been Africanized over the past 20 years, these institutions are only beginning to become indigenous in values, priorities, and power relationships. With few exceptions, the rule of law and constitutional procedure gives way to more direct forms of personal and group power whenever strains develop within the system. Since national institutions, including political parties, are generally subject to the twin pressures of corruption and manipulation by top–level political elites, most institutions are weak. The organs of state economic, administrative, and military power are politicized. Few African states have developed political systems that allow continuing and peaceful changes of leadership. Thus, political institutions are underdeveloped. These factors have consequences for regional order.

The politico–military climate in Africa is profoundly dependent upon external powers and the balance of relationships among them. In the past the UN system, the continuing European presence, and a fair degree of reciprocal U.S.–Soviet restraint have all served to buffer Africa from the consequences of weakness and dependence. Major internationalized conflicts were, until the mid–1970s, relatively infrequent when judged against the enormous potential for conflict (see below). Relatively few conflicts became militarized to a substantial degree, and Africa's share of world arms imports remained low as did African military spending. With only a few exceptions (North Africa, the Horn, Nigeria, and South Africa and Zimbabwe), African armies were not capable of sustained effort against

serious resistance, whether against internal or external threats. Training, morale, logistics and maintenance, and communications were the principal military shortcomings, apart from the modest size and minimal hardware of the forces themselves.

The 5 years since the Portuguese revolution have underscored Africa's military dependence, assuring that African regional politics would reflect the evolving external balance. A number of conflicts have become militarized as Africans are now arming themselves at an unprecedented rate. This process of militarization has occurred at the explicit initiative of African governments and guerrilla groups; as in the past, however, it is to external rather than internal (i.e., African) decision makers that one must look for an explanation of the growth of armies and hardware inventories.

The new factor since Portugal's departure from its colonies is not the African propensity to seek outside support for one side or another in conflict situations; this tendency has many antecedents in history. Rather, the new factor is an imbalance in the willingness of the Western and communist powers to respond to African requests and to exploit opportunities for politico-military influence. The very fact of this imbalance — in the past 3 years, Moscow and its allies account for between two-thirds and three-quarters of African arms imports — fosters further African arms requests and the growth of security concerns. For the first time since the Congo (Zaire) crises of the early 1960s, the continent has become a major arena of external rivalries and ambitions without, however, lessening the continuing fact of dependence. In fact, it can be argued that the growing amounts and sophistication of arms imports into Africa only further underline the need for outside training and support.

On the other hand, African leaders have a realistic appreciation of the extent and implications of this dependent regional order. The charter of the OAU represents the best efforts of African diplomacy to provide a politico-legal basis for security (both national and regional), in the absence of an African capacity to provide for politico-military security. The OAU principles of territorial integrity (within inherited borders), political independence, non-interference in internal affairs, and non-alignment are, first and foremost, security principles aimed at managing the impact of regional weakness. The OAU's tol-

erance of external defense ties and its failure to move beyond conciliation procedures to peace–keeping forces simply recognizes the region's realities.

To criticize the OAU's weakness as an institution for maintaining order is to criticize the member states themselves. Since the mid–1970s, the OAU system has at times been reduced to the role of an impotent bystander, prepared to ratify whatever faits accompli emerge on the ground. At the same time, the regional organization remains an African–controlled device capable of moderating polarization through diplomatic pressure and able, on occasion, to lessen divisions that might otherwise break open into a renewed "scramble for Africa." However divided African states are over the Western response to the 1978 Shaba crisis or over the Tanzanian role in ousting Idi Amin in Uganda, it seems likely that division and conflict would be still less restrained in the absence of the OAU, as a forum and diplomatic coordinating and legitimating device. While the organization has not been capable of raising and deploying its own peace–keeping forces, it has acted to sanction modest military cooperation among member states that might otherwise intensify conflicts and insecurity.

The African regional order is in transition from the post–colonial system (1960–1974) in which Western influence was the predominant external factor to an as yet undefined system. While African leaders show little enthusiasm for replacing Western with communist predominance, neither they nor the OAU organisms are capable by themselves of preventing this from happening.

In a transitional period, it is not surprising that individual states and leaders would have divergent interpretations of the balance of forces on the continent. The Angolan civil conflict split OAU members 22–22 until the outcome was decided by force of arms and on the ground. Nigeria, as one of Africa's most secure states, is better able than most to afford the luxury of warning both the Soviets and the West against military over–involvement in Africa. Tanzania's reaction to the Western–African operation in Zaire, on the other hand, suggests that some kinds of foreign intervention are more acceptable than others; the key factor for President Julius K. Nyerere is, apparently, the legitimacy of the existing government being defended. Tanzania's successful drive to unseat the Ugandan re-

gime of Amin may signal the beginning of an era in which OAU principles are interpreted with increasing national discretion.

Another aspect of the current transition in Africa is the growing disparity in military strength among African states. Tanzania's success in Uganda can be explained in part by the rapid disintegration of Amin's forces, but it is also clear that Tanzania's military superiority was possible because Amin did not receive effective sustained external support. Elsewhere in Africa, disparities in power will continue to develop. Nigeria's role in Chad (as well as Libya's, which helped prompt it) could point to a broader pattern. The capacity of Morocco and Egypt, together with several weaker Francophone states, to support friendly governments is another variant of this pattern. In some cases, imbalances will occur because non–African military support is withheld from a threatened state or government, while in others the provision of such support may create an imbalance unless it is matched on the other side. Both cases point to a new military climate in which African disparities fuel African security concerns that, in turn, fuel the search for outside patrons. When the major outside powers disagree about the rules of competition in Africa, the potential instability is magnified.

Leaders who are nervous about Soviet intentions in Africa may find it nonetheless impossible to oppose publicly communist support of southern Africa guerrilla groups unless clear–cut diplomatic options exist. But the depth of their security concern is no less real, and will predictably lead to a growing list of African states seeking Western military support and arms. The current militarization of Africa has its own logic, based on the reality of conflict and weakness in a global environment of unstable big power relationships. Three types of conflict — southern African insurgency; political collapse in weak states; and cross–border conflicts over transport, resource, and boundary issues — suggest a range of possible openings for continued Soviet–Cuban involvement.

Decolonization Struggles: Southern Africa and the Sahara

Despite apparent differences, there are important structural similarities between southern African conflicts and the Polisario struggle against Morocco (formerly allied with Mauri-

tania) in the former Spanish Sahara. In the Sahara, as in Zimbabwe and Namibia, the question of who has the "right" to decolonize a territory, and how, continues as a central issue. The recourse to arms by guerrilla movements hinders the diplomacy of compromise and pre–emption. The obduracy of incumbent, de facto authorities fosters the recourse to arms. In the absence of generally accepted legitimacy, communist–armed guerrillas with or without proxy forces gain the necessary opening to create legitimacy through diplomatic efforts and superior force. The Angolan precedent not only fosters the recourse to arms by groups that succeed in appealing to Moscow, but it also fosters the impression that Soviet (and allied) support will prove to be more decisive than any other kind.

Three types of outcomes are possible in such circumstances: surrender by incumbent authorities, assuming there is a unified entity to which surrender or terms can be offered; a drawn out conflict reflecting a rough balance of external support offered to the warring parties; or successful mediation backed by alternative instruments of security and order. To date, the Sahara conflict approximates the second of these possibilities, but it appears that the ultimate outcome may be shaped by the broader context of evolving Moroccan–Algerian relations and Moroccan domestic stability.

The southern African cases differ from those of the Sahara in that incumbent authorities in Namibia and Zimbabwe have been unsuccessful in acquiring even the legitimacy of Morocco–in–Sahara. External political and military support for their preferred transition schemes has not, so far, been available, however much the Western powers may prefer moderate outcomes to "revolutionary" ones. Superficially, the conflicts concern the nature of legitimate change. In substance, however, there are African parties with incompatible aspirations over the core issue of who will hold power in the successor state and with what kinds of outside relationships. The role of local white minorities becomes a "swing" issue in the conflict, to the extent that whites seek to shape the transition; but the underlying question is whether "gradualists" or "revolutionaries" will take over.

Interestingly, the diplomacy of Zimbabwe and Namibia suggests that it is the African frontline states and the Western powers that care least about what kind of governments emerge

from the struggles, so long as the process of escalating violence is terminated before further damage is done to vital interests. But African frontline freedom of maneuver has been limited by the presence of heavily armed guerrilla groups (and foreign advisors) that may no longer be easily controlled. Western flexibility is sharply constrained by a self–imposed unwillingness either to compete with the communist powers in supporting guerrilla movements or to support any transition proposals that do not receive guerrilla and frontline state support.

Meanwhile, guerrilla movements neatly combine the goals of liberation and power, thereby facilitating the acquisition of international recognition, arms, and a substantial measure of diplomatic veto power during the transitional period. Their principal constraints are twofold: to avoid being hurried into settlements that threaten or question their coming to power; and to retain the backing of African hosts and communist arms suppliers. The case of Zimbabwe illustrates this imperative. Instead of external powers competing for influence with the various internal and external nationalist factions, the factions are themselves competing to align themselves with whomever is most reliably committed to the pursuit of the struggle. In current circumstances, the nationalist factions are obliged to choose between the white establishment internally and the Soviet–Cuban presence externally. Unless the Western powers and the People's Republic of China modify their current stance and commit real resources to these conflicts (or devise more promising diplomatic approaches), guerrilla movements and host states will be increasingly unable to avoid the logic of outright alliance with the only available source of armed power. Assuming that Soviet–backed guerrillas come to power in one or more of these territories, dependence on Moscow will not end quickly. As Angola demonstrates, a forceful seizure of power from armed opponents may only increase the dependence of a new regime on the external patrons who helped it gain power.

Moscow and its allies face their own limitations, however. While supporting the path of armed struggle at a level adequate to retain primacy as the military champion of liberation, the USSR must appear to operate within the framework of OAU norms and sensibilities. Where diplomatic avenues remain open, Moscow can be expected to move cautiously so as to reduce direct responsibility for bloody outcomes. Though its

subsequent leverage over successor regimes may be directly proportional to the level of violence they require to gain power, Soviet and African state interests begin to diverge at the point where regional disruption and violent methods become ends in themselves. Finally, and probably most important, African gains must be viewed by Moscow in a context of global interests that include a desire to avoid stirring up a determined Western reaction.

The coming months will witness decisive events in the unfolding of a new southern African balance as Zimbabwean and Namibian developments move to a head. At stake are not only the orientation of successor governments in these territories, but the regional role of South Africa, the nature of the guerrilla threat capable of being mounted against the republic, the outcome of the Angolan civil war, and the fate of economic and political systems in neighboring black states — especially those of Botswana, Zambia, and Mozambique. While the range of possible outcomes is vast, the relative roles played by military power and diplomacy will determine the degree of influence Moscow and its allies gain in the new sub–regional order. No combination of Western, Chinese, and moderate Arab influence will check Soviet–Cuban activity if the key factor shaping transition is military power, for the simple reason that external military factors are so asymmetrically in favor of Moscow. With strong Western backing, it is conceivable that UN or African forces could forestall communist faits accompli based on armed strength on the ground. But the African states, including Nigeria, remain unable to act independently in shaping the new pattern of southern African relationships.

Consequently, African leaders will be obliged increasingly to face up to hard choices on the road to majority rule. Their willingness to cooperate with Western diplomatic and military initiatives will be a measure of African influence in shaping the new order. The alternative for African leaders will be to become bystanders as guerrilla groups and their communist military patrons gain increasing initiative. To the extent that force rather than diplomacy gains the upper hand, black states in southern Africa will no longer be able to afford the luxury of superficial alignments and "orientations" in external relationships. Such alignments will be based not on abstract principles

but on the facts of regional power, dependency patterns, and transportation and economic linkages.

South Africa's military and diplomatic posture will also play a major role in shaping the new southern African balance. On the one hand, Pretoria appears to recognize that it does not have the diplomatic capital to shape the Namibian and Zimbabwean outcome by itself; moreover, it will not lightly accept the risk of sharply increased Western pressure, including possible sanctions. Its preferred scenario clearly is to engage the Western powers in the search for regional accommodations that may reduce the risk of increased communist military influence and an accelerated guerrilla build–up on its borders. On the other hand, there remain limits on Pretoria's readiness for further substantial concessions in Namibia; and there is no reason to suppose that South African forces would stand by if Cuban forces joined the fray in Zimbabwe, especially if Western sentiments were divided, as seems likely. South Africa will seek to keep its options open as long as possible, but cannot be counted on to cooperate or back down in the face of outside pressure. The power equation in southern Africa gives the republic some room to maneuver in the coming year or two.

Looking further ahead, the burgeoning South African military build–up assures that Pretoria will retain military superiority in southern Africa against all challenges — apart from a substantially increased communist ground force commitment — for some time to come. This imbalance itself means that guerrilla groups and neighboring states will increasingly shop around for security patrons, while the growth of guerrilla capabilities directed against the republic will increase the security issues posed to neighboring states. African leaders will not abandon their support for violent means to achieve change or revolution in South Africa. But the tactics and timing of African pressure for change will depend overwhelmingly on (a) the nature of change in Namibia and Zimbabwe and (b) the willingness of Western nations to play a security and diplomatic role in the region.

Political Collapse of Weak States

Weak states abound in contemporary Africa, for reasons indicated under "Elements of the African Regional Order"

above. Until recently, this weakness has been accepted, by Africans and outsiders, as a fact of life in a modernizing region. Weakness both has meant and has resulted from (a) a failure to tackle effectively the awesome human and economic problems of development and (b) and unstable political structure characterized by frequent coups and cabinet shuffles, which had relatively little impact on the basic administrative–economic system. Vulnerability was too generalized to be easily exploited, and outside influences worked gently but effectively to reinforce stability rather than to disrupt it.

This pattern has changed in three ways. First, a far larger volume of arms and money has become available to movements and regimes with an interest in challenging the existing order. The Soviet build–up of Somalia's offensive capacity up to 1977, at a time of mounting disarray in Ethiopia, is but one example. Zaire, Chad, and Mauritania have also experienced growing military pressure from movements that, unlike the exile movements of the 1960s, are now in a position to challenge incumbent governments seriously. The arms and funds that have made this possible come either directly from Soviet and allied sources or from their key African security partners, which serve as channels or funnels. In part, this is accounted for by Soviet and Cuban policy decisions aimed at destabilizing pro–Western regimes or at raising the cost to Western powers of continuing their links with them. The militarization of long–festering tensions has also been affected by the growing, competitive role of militant and moderate Arab governments anxious to pursue or defend their interests in the increasingly vulnerable African environment.

Second, the great majority of African states, and especially the weaker ones, have been confronted with severe economic adjustment problems in the wake of oil price rises and global recession. The weaker states (e.g., most of the landlocked Francophone states — Zaire, Uganda, Ethiopia, Zambia, Benin, Congo–Brazzaville) have been least able to adjust to the income effect of these outside pressures, thereby aggravating dependency on traditional patrons or necessitating a switch to new ones more willing to pay the price of patronage.

Third, and for the first time, a marked asymmetry has emerged between the pragmatic, flexible Western approach toward support of shaky governments and the readiness of

communist powers to lend decisive physical support to governments facing major civil crisis. The Ugandan case, however, suggests that there are definite limits to Moscow's willingness to back regimes that become isolated from most elements of the population.

The overall effect of these changes has been to dramatize the contrast between the approaches pursued by Western and communist powers in Africa and to underline the distinction between have and have-not states. Military versus developmental approaches toward regime security have come into increasingly sharp contrast; external powers committed to a developmental policy in Africa are, by the same token, expected to find a larger pool of resources than was required in the earlier period. The cases of Mauritania, Chad, Niger, Ethiopia, Uganda, Zaire, Zambia, Angola, and Botswana demonstrate, in one way or another, the new choices Africans face.

To these problems should be added the situation of politically ossified regimes — whether monarchical or republican — that appear unable to change except through revolutionary processes. The imperial Ethiopian government may be but one example of the syndrome. Revolution, in the African context, could imply class, ethnic, regional, or cultural-religious dissidence. What is new in the current period is that such dissidence becomes legitimate when external powers and the OAU or UN systems are unwilling to support the existing order and when the potency of the threat is steadily growing. New "facts" on the ground develop their own momentum when most local and external parties confine themselves to the role of observers, rather than participants. Zaire, Chad, and the Central African Empire could follow the pattern, while questions must be raised over the longer term about such borderline countries as Morocco, Senegal, Guinea, the Ivory Coast, Congo–Brazzaville, and Swaziland.

Political collapse, as the Iranian case demonstrates, is not only found in states that are objectively "weak." Stated another way, the definition of weakness may vary over time and place. Twenty–five–to 30–year–old governments such as that of the National party in South Africa, the Neo–Destourian autocracy of Tunisia, or post–Neguib Egypt may also be vulnerable to at least temporary political upheaval, offering openings to external manipulaltion.

However, for analytical purposes it is preferable to focus attention on states whose political, economic, and institutional weaknesses suggest their "ungovernability," rather than their internal conflicts. The distinction between ineffective systems and contested ones is important because the former are more vulnerable to a wider range of threats. While the line between the two types of weakness may become blurred, there is an obvious contrast between the vulnerability of Zaire and that of South Africa or Egypt. A wider range of pretexts is available to the dissidents (and their patrons) when the issue is not which group governs but whether any group is governing. The distinction, however, does not point to a prescription for U.S. policy. It simply indicates that Africa's ungovernability problem may be a lasting element of the environment in which U.S. interests are pursued.

Resource, Transport, and Boundary Conflicts

This broad category of potential conflicts might, at first glance, appear to be so analytically diffuse as to be without substance. What is implied, however, is conflict over scarce and tangible assets that are in short supply in contemporary Africa: money (including Libyan and Saudi–style political subsidies, as well as straightforward development aid); land; subsoil minerals; transport linkages and leverage; and ocean access. In the early post–independence years, a number of outside observers pointed to Africa's territorial legacy of illogical divisions as a minefield of future crises.

Such forecasts appear to have been premature or ill–conceived. Few African boundary conflicts have yet become militarized; those that have — in the Horn, Chad, and the Maghreb — represent special cases in the overall African context. They are special because of the far higher level of military strength that makes possible the periodic outbreak of major conflict, and because the boundary legacy from colonial times is contested. The majority of border disputes have not arisen over territorial–irredentist ambitions or over conflicting historical claims, since the European boundary legacy is generally accepted. Disputes have centered on the implementation of sovereignty over borders, which did not previously bar the free flow of people, animals, and goods. Second, frontier conflict has

arisen where boundaries consist of little more than lines on a map and over ambiguities in the intent of former colonial administrators. Third, geopolitical concerns have been aroused by the discovery of raw material deposits and by the heightened vulnerability of many national economies to transport dependency on neighboring states as transport requirements grow.

In all such cases, the common element has been a broader setting of accepted (OAU) principles, military weakness, and minimal external willingness to stir up African territorial issues. There have always been two possible approaches to the management of Africa's territorial and economic balkanization: cooperation in joint institutions and projects or security-conscious competition along more autarchic lines. In the 1974–1978 period, the two approaches have had an uneasy coexistence. There is disturbing evidence, however, that the politics of boundaries, transport, and resources are becoming entwined with life and death issues of regime security, economic and political collapse, and guerrilla operations. In central and southern Africa, it is no longer possible to make neat distinctions among the various roots of turmoil. Soviet arms flows fuel guerrilla activity oriented against both black and white minority governments. As the balance between guerrillas and black government security forces moves steadily in favor of the former, the latter are increasingly anxious to broaden their security options.

Thus, in Zaire, Zambia, Malawi, and Botswana, moderate governments with frail economies face increasingly severe dilemmas of regime security, heightened by the politics of transportation. As the Zimbabwean and Namibian conflicts continue, the same pattern could begin to affect Mozambique and Angola. The potential for guerrilla blackmail over transport routes further narrows government options, forcing some governments to face up to dependency choices that could be avoided or blurred in the earlier period. The capacity of South African and Zimbabwean forces to strike at guerrilla camps with impunity adds to the pressures for militarization of neighboring states.

It is too early to forecast the outcome of trends identified in this section. Key factors will be the outcome of current struggles over Zimbabwe and Namibia: the response of Western

powers and their friends to African economic and security needs; the extent of South African pragmatism in developing and maintaining workable relationships with black neighbors; and the willingness of the latter to work constructively with the former. A worse case scenario could envisage years of continuing civil and cross–border strife in the zone from Zaire to South Africa with dire results for moderate black governments, mineral investment and output, and all forms of interstate cooperation. But this prospect is by no means inevitable. Moreover, it seems relatively unlikely that boundary conflicts, as traditionally conceived, will play as large a role as the struggle by African leaders to gain some measure of control over their political and economic fortunes.

Prospects for Regional Security

While African nationalist sensitivities over foreign influence and white minority rule continue to grow, the ability of African states — individually and collectively — to shape a new African regional order is declining. That is because African states are not united in their other regional goals or on the tactics of liberation; African states are buffered from foreign influence and intervention only (a) when they restrain themselves from inviting it and (b) when there is some degree of balance and restraint in the policies of external actors.

There is no reason to posit an increase in the strength of the OAU as a mediating or peace–keeping institution in these circumstances. The influence of the organization will be a function of the extent to which diplomatic, rather than military, instruments are used in Africa. By the same token, the capacity of the OAU to serve as a nationalist check on foreign intervention will, ironically, depend upon the degree of disparity or, alternatively, balance in the African postures adopted by outside powers. What the OAU can continue to do to foster security will be confined principally to legitimizing the diplomatic and security efforts undertaken by the stronger African states. It would, therefore, be interesting to know which states will be capable of taking such initiatives and what their external orientation will be in the coming period. Taking the July 1978 OAU summit as a point of reference, it can be projected that the major states and blocs will continue to include: the moderate

Arab African states (the Sudan, Egypt, and Morocco); the frontline "radicals" and their more distant friends in Algeria, Libya, and Ethiopia; Nigeria, in a class more or less by itself; the numerically substantial moderate–to–conconservative bloc of weaker states (both Anglophone and Francophone); and the geopolitically swing states, whose internal strains make them the objects, rather than the leaders, of African political initiatives (Zaire, Chad, Uganda, Zambia, Botswana, and Angola).

These divisions add up to a highly complex arena for policy making by outsiders. Relatively few states have the military strength or financial resources to involve themselves in cooperative military undertakings with external powers unless the latter cover virtually all costs and provide total logistic back–up. Some states are unwilling to participate in such ventures except under UN auspices, while others are suspicious of the "neutrality" and big power influence inherent in UN operations. If outsiders decide to operate with their closest African partners outside the OAU or UN frameworks, they obtain the advantages of freedom of action and assured military results (at least in the short term). On the other hand, they also incur the costs of possible African (majority OAU) hostility and may end up bearing open–ended military burdens that cannot be effectively assumed by Africans themselves.

The preceding analysis indicates that Africa will continue to present a conflicting and confusing puzzle to Western policy makers. Regional instability and local threats will remain commonplace. Less clear will be the level of attraction that African trouble spots will have for Soviet and Cuban policy makers. Equally unclear, when dealing at the continental level, is which kinds of instability should be viewed as most worrisome by Washington.

Before addressing the Soviet–Cuban dimensions of the problem, it is useful to bear in mind several general conclusions about the African policy climate. First, change itself is not the problem; in some cases change is clearly a precondition of a more stable climate. Second, it matters from the regional and global standpoint how change takes place. Third, military conflict is less the cause than the symptom of underlying instability or strain. No amount of external military input can resolve, by itself, conflicts or problems that threaten Western interests.

Yet, once a conflict has become militarized, it is unlikely to be solved by non–military means or to be "de-militarized" unless there are alternative means that address the security dimension of the problem. In some cases, this means that a balance of military power will be required before meaningful negotiation can occur. Fourth, the very complexity of African political conflict requires that selectivity and discrimination be applied in dealing with them. This, however, does not imply that every African crisis can be explained away by reference to special, one–country factors, particularly when Soviet–Cuban activity has played an important role. Given the nature of our competitive relationship with the communist powers, it is legitimate to focus on the extent of such involvement.

II. THE SOVIET OFFENSIVE IN AFRICA*

Few international developments in recent years have been as disturbing to the United States as the new Soviet political and military offensive in Africa. It is there that the USSR, for the first time, demonstrated to the world its ability and willingness to act as a decisive and assertive global power. The Soviet intervention in Angola was probably the single most important development in shifting U.S. foreign policy consensus from support of détente, as it was formulated under Richard Nixon and Henry Kissinger in 1972–1973. There is little doubt that Soviet African activities in the late 1970s were not just a meaningless accident based strictly on the unique circumstances of a regional political terrain. Rather, the Soviet behavior reflected a transformation of the USSR from essentially a continental power into a true superpower with a growing global reach, determined to make and, to a considerable degree, capable of making an important input in the formation of a world order.

Nevertheless, recognition of the fundamental Soviet ambitions to establish a global presence and to alter the international status quo formulated by others more in accordance with Moscow's geopolitical interests leaves unanswered a number of crucial questions regarding Soviet motives, intentions, and plans. To start with, there is a debate as to whether Soviet performance in Africa represents some well–defined policy developed specifically for this continent or whether Africa, for a variety of reasons, simply happens to be a convenient testing ground for some more general trends in the Kremlin's foreign policy. Another important issue also creating a great controversy is to what extent Soviet African exploits reveal a well–thought–out design and to what extent they are an outcome of opportunities that the Soviets, due to their newly acquired sea-and airlift capabilities, coupled with perceived American unwillingness to become involved, could not resist exploring. Finally, there is a problem of continuity in Soviet African policy. While there are certainly new elements in Soviet conduct south of the Sahara, it is more difficult to establish exactly how they fit into the general evolutionary development of Soviet policy toward Africa.

---

* The principal contributor to this section was Dimitri Simes.

The Evolution of Soviet Policy

Despite its high visibility and costs, recent Soviet involvement in sub–Saharan Africa is not a product of a major policy reassessment in Moscow giving a particular priority to this region. Africa was upgraded, both in absolute terms and relative to other areas. Still, in the overall Soviet foreign policy framework, the share of material resources and attention it gets from the Soviet leadership is still greater only than that of Australia and Latin America. Soviet African policy seems to be an integral component of Moscow's diplomacy vis–à–vis the Third World. Besides the reliance on the Cubans, there is not much unique about Soviet behavior in Africa. A growing boldness in applying force; a new and less conservative assessment of risks; a refusal to subordinate regional interests to the requirements of bilateral relations with the United States, or, for that matter, with the West in general; an attempt to position itself as a champion of Third World causes; and an aggressive competition with Western and Chinese influence — all of these essential characteristics of Soviet performance in areas of international instability are in no sense limited to Africa.

The Soviet pattern of encouraging and making possible the use of force in Third World conflict did not start with Africa. India's successful offensive against Pakistan in 1971 would hardly have been possible without massive supplies of Soviet armaments, as well as the Kremlin's political support. A Soviet naval task force was moved close to the confrontation area presumably in order to pre–empt the West from using its naval power as a political weapon to pressure India. Even earlier, Soviet pilots took part in combat in Yeman in 1967 and in Egypt in 1970. And it is well–known that the USSR supplied the Vietnamese with massive aid and gave them a protective political umbrella for the invasion of Cambodia in December 1978. The above–mentioned situations — where a limited assistance was made available — cannot, however, be equated with military intervention in African conflicts, directly by proxy, in effect determining their outcome. The difference between sending a handful of pilots and 40 thousand Cubans, including combat units armed, trained, and delivered by the USSR, is obvious and cannot be ignored.

Nevertheless, this greater Soviet willingness to use force

does not necessarily reflect an unusual emphasis on Africa. Rather, it may be connected with the particular utility of limited military effort in the African context, on the one hand, and the lesser risk of provoking the United States into a confrontation posture, on the other. There is little evidence that, as far as Moscow is concerned, there is anything justifying a special focus on Africa, except that it offers excellent opportunities to expand Soviet influence at a relatively low cost. Consequently, future Soviet activities south of the Sahara will depend: (1) on the developments in this region; (2) on opportunities somewhere else, probably in areas perceived more crucial to Soviet international interests and having priority in claiming Moscow's military and political commitment; and (3) on the extent to which the cost remains low, in terms either of Western response or of African reactions.

Soviet resources are not unlimited. The current economic slowdown imposes on the Kremlin the necessity to make choices in pursuing those foreign policy objectives that require a significant material investment. The Soviet leadership cannot disregard the simple fact of life that simultaneously taking care of the security of such clients as Angola, Ethiopia, Afghanistan, and Vietnam, as well as Cuba inevitably demands cuts from other military and civilian programs.

To what degree the persistent tendency to exploit opportunities in the Third World amounts to some sort of grand design or is essentially reactive is not a question allowing one–dimensional yes or no answers. In terms of consequences for the West, it makes little short–term difference whether the Kremlin has some well–thought–out strategy toward Africa or simply capitalizes on numerous instabilities and turmoils. What really matters is that the Soviet leadership has a strong predisposition to define what represents opportunities in Africa and essentially everywhere in the Third World through a prism that, among other considerations, is heavily colored by perceptions of fundamental East–West contradictions.

Moscow's record indicates that, as far as the Soviet elite is concerned, a zero–sum game, where a loss for one competitor is automatically a gain for another, still dominates the rules of the competition for power, influence, and resources in the Third World. Africa is just another integral component in the Soviet world outlook, viewing America's international presence as the

single most important obstacle to channeling change in a direction favorable to Soviet interests and values. This is not to suggest that from the Soviet standpoint, rivalry with the United States, or even with the West in general, is the only global challenge to Moscow's advances. It is preoccupied with China as well.

The Kremlin is also aware of the growing multipolarity and complexity of the world order, where an exclusive focus on dealing with one opponent may have considerable costs and many missed opportunities. But the subtlety of the way in which the zero–sum game is interpreted in Moscow indicates the growing sophistication, maturity, and pragmatism of Soviet foreign policy in the 1970s, rather than a new willingness to accept the notion that some form of American global role should be implicitly accepted and unchallenged. Accordingly, it appears that any reduction in the U.S. presence, any jeopardy to U.S. prestige, or any humiliation of the United States is perceived by the Soviet political class with such satisfaction that occasionally there is a willingness to hurt American positions even when there is a realistic possibility that the USSR itself would not benefit — indeed would also be hurt — by developments Moscow attempts to encourage. Iran provides a perfect illustration of this mindset in the Kremlin.

While a discussion of Soviet policy toward the revolution in Iran does not belong to this paper, it is still useful to note that the USSR launched a major campaign against the shah primarily because of his American connection. This was done despite the fact that under the shah Iran had a fairly stable political relationship with the Soviet Union, was involved in massive economic cooperation with it (including important supplies of Iranian natural gas), and was on the top of the list of Soviet arms recipients (and, unlike many, paid in hard cash). The immediate alternative to the shah was not the pro–Moscow forces, but the Moslem fundamentalists, hardly appealing to a Soviet regime concerned with nationality and religious problems inside the USSR. But a desire to oust the Washington-oriented shah outweighed all these concerns.

The Soviet Union still views itself as an underdog having to catch up with the United States in the world arena. As a rising superpower, the USSR feels a need to be highly visible and to establish a record of success around the globe, to prove to

everyone, including itself, that it is indeed in the same league with the United States.

The Soviets constantly complain that, while U.S.–Soviet documents signed in 1972–1973 recognize the USSR as equal to the United States, Washington is unwilling to live with the consequences of parity. The Soviets see an element of a double standard in the U.S. denial to Moscow of the right to act in a manner threatening the international status quo, which is thought to be inherently unacceptable to the Kremlin. Soviet officials claim that there is a clear contradiction in American declaratory policy, recognizing the Soviet Union as an equal and acting in what is considered impulsive opposition to Moscow's behaving as a superpower. They claim to be offended by Washington's protests against Soviet advances, even in areas outside the American system of alliances and never known to be of particular concern to the United States. As reported by the Soviet leadership's official spokesman, Leonid Zamyatin, Leonid Brezhnev personally communicated to President Carter in Vienna in June 1979 that Moscow is "quite surprised at the ease with which in the United States some sphere of the earth far from the United States is proclaimed a sphere of vital interests of the United States."

Soviet Foreign Minister Andrey Gromyko adequately represented the Soviet viewpoint when he declared that no longer can any significant international crisis be solved without Soviet participation or against Soviet interests. In this context African engagements appeal to Moscow by offering a good chance to behave as a legitimate member of the superpower club, to be reckoned with in all global developments.

The Soviet intererst in Africa has a long history. Soon after the Bolshevik revolution, the Soviets made an effort to establish contacts with radical movements of African and Asian countries. Before the mid–1950s, these ties were embryonic and of little political significance. Nikita Khrushchev was confronted unexpectedly with a new phenomenon, unanticipated by Marxist–Leninist theory, of an emergence of new independent states in Africa and Asia, many of them quite hostile to their previous colonial masters. There was much excitement in Moscow regarding the great potential of a "historic alliance" between the Soviet bloc and the newly liberated nations. The collapse of the colonial system was interpreted by Soviet

theoreticians as a sign that the capitalist system had entered the third and, in all likelihood, the final stage of its crisis. The fascination in Moscow with so–called "revolutionary democrats," who were expected to become faithful allies of the Soviets and pave the road to a "truly socialist transformation" of their societies, was partly based on an assumption that post–colonial nations were bound gradually to choose the Soviet model of development and adopt an increasingly anti–Western posture. Most of these hopes were already proved unjustified by events in Indonesia, Ghana, Egypt, etc., in the 1960s, and Moscow seriously reassessed its enthusiasm regarding both the pace and irreversibility of change in the Third World.

Eventually, Soviet analysts came to the conclusion that there was a growing polarization leading to "two diametrically opposite trends" among the community of developing nations, some of which were moving closer to the USSR while others were increasingly integrated, as suggested by Evgenii M. Primakov, director of the influential Soviet Institute of Oriental Studies, not only in "the world capitalist economy but also in the system of imperialist politics."

After many disappointments in the Third World, the Soviets are careful not to overestimate the commitment to Marxism–Leninism in developing nations. After burning their hands several times, Soviet analysts, unlike some of their Western colleagues, are extremely cautious in not creating the impression that countries like Angola, Ethiopia, and Mozambique already satisfy criteria for acceptance as communist. For instance, according to Rostislav Ulyanovsky, a distinguished Soviet Third World expert and deputy chief of the Communist party Central Committee, International Department, the commitment of African revolutionaries to "scientific socialism" should be taken with a grain of salt. "Although they sound sincere," he warns, "one must bear in mind that their Marxism–Leninism has not been put to the test, that at times it has no adequate social and party basis, that it is sometimes merely reduced to borrowed formulas and is not the flesh and bone of the people, the working masses, the leadership itself." Thus Ulyanovsky advises not to be hasty with conclusions about the strength and longevity of the devotion of African states to Marxism–Leninism. Significantly, despite the socialist rhetoric of some African statesmen, sophisticated Soviet

observers suggest that it is uncertain whether any among these African countries has moved to the stage of so–called "people's democratic revolution," which is considered a fundamental step in "non–capitalist development." Angola and Mozambique are mentioned as the two principal hopefuls in this respect. Yet even in those cases, Soviet analysis includes a cautionary "perhaps."

This hopeful but reserved tone is in striking contrast to the uncritical enthusiasm with which the Soviet Union welcomed African nationalism in the late 1950s and early 1960s. Since the mid–1960s, Moscow has reduced its involvement south of the Sahara, because of disillusionment with a lack of rapid progress in Africa; new, appealing, but at the same time costly, opportunities elsewhere, particularly in the Middle East; and commitments to Vietnam. The new stage of the Soviet presence in Africa started with the collapse of the Portuguese colonial empire in 1974.

The Instruments of Soviet Power

While fundamental Soviet objectives in Africa probably have not changed very much, the means Moscow employs in its pursuit of them are different in many respects. First, the whole Soviet perception of African development has gone through a considerable modification. For the first time, the USSR is in a position of having regimes claiming their devotion to Marxism–Leninism. There is a certain skepticism in Moscow about the dependability of their commitment to scientific socialism and an alliance with Moscow; still, the Kremlin cannot but feel more comfortable dealing with nations willing to adopt — even if only rhetorically — the Soviet model. Since some of the self–proclaimed African Marxist–Leninist states enjoy respect and influence on the continent, the Soviet Union as their patron and friend is a beneficiary by association.

The USSR takes a more differentiated approach in Africa than in the 1950s and 1960s, distinguishing between states like Angola and Ethiopia, led by parties of "revolutionary vanguard," and those that rely on market forces, a degree of political pluralism, and often cooperation with the West. Soviet observers seem to accept that some African nations, contrary to earlier expectations, may choose a capitalist path of devel-

opment, not as a brief transitional stage, but as a long–term economic, social, and political option. Consequently, it is the former group that is perceived in Moscow as a major Soviet hope on the African continent.

Second, there is a difference in emphasis as far as Soviet aid to Africa is concerned. The focus now is clearly on military assistance rather than economic cooperation. From 1972 to 1976 all Soviet arms transfers to the Third World doubled; in the case of Africa they increased almost 20 times, from $55 million to over $1 billion — even before the Soviets invested more than $1 billion in military aid to Ethiopia. The greater focus on influencing Africa through arms supplies affects both Soviet perceptions of opportunities on the continent and the perceptions of local actors regarding the availability of outside help if they choose to rely on military solutions. In short, not only has the USSR developed a stake in a continuing turmoil in Africa but, by making weapons, advisors, and even combat units available, it encourages competing African factions to think more in terms of military than of political options, and consequently to display less flexibility in a search for compromises with their internal opponents or disagreeable neighbors.

Third, the Soviet Union is more willing than ever to get involved directly or by proxy. The Soviets were traditionally conservative in projecting force to non–contiguous areas. This was partly a result, of course, of the lack of sufficient sea– and airlift capabilities. Nevertheless, there had to be, in addition to an upgrading of an ability to project power, a political reassessment of the risks involved before the pragmatic and usually unimaginative Soviet leadership would accept the current level of Soviet military presence. In November 1975, during the civil war in Angola, the Soviets stationed a contingent of marines on their ships off the Congolese coast, to provide security for landing supplies to the Popular Movement for the Liberation of Angola (PMLA). Still, Moscow kept a fairly low profile in Angola, limiting its intervention to delivering Cuban advisors and units.

In Ethiopia, the Soviet presence was more obvious. Four Soviet generals, including Army General Vasily Petrov, then first deputy commander–in–chief of the Soviet ground forces, were coordinating the Ethiopian offensive. There were also scores of instructors, technicians, and other support personnel.

The Soviet potential to project power ashore on a large scale against hostile forces will improve substantially. If current U.S. projections are correct, the Soviet Union is going to build at least eight of the *Kiev*–class anti–submarine carriers, plus a new generation of large–deck, nuclear–powered aircraft carriers. Furthermore, this growing capability is being complemented by the newest Soviet amphibious ship, the *Ivan Rokov*, already used during Soviet naval maneuvers in combination with the *Kiev*–class mini–carriers.

Finally, the Soviets today make a far greater use of proxies. This habit of relying on client states to run errands for Moscow is not something new. Czechoslovakia fronted for the Kremlin on supplying arms to Gamal Abdel Nasser in the mid–1950s. East Germans arrived in Africa to advise local security forces more than a decade ago. However, the emergence of a 40 thousand–strong Cuban force brings this trend to a qualitatively new level.

There is a danger in overemphasizing the independent motives of Cuba, the German Democratic Republic, and other Soviet clients in their African pursuits. When Adolf Hitler's armies invaded Russia in 1941, they included Finnish and Romanian forces, each of which had their own quite legitimate grievances vis–à–vis the Soviet Union. Their objectives in the war were different from those of the Germans. But this did not matter much from the Soviet military's planners' standpoint. The Finns and the Romanians were part of the invasion and had to be treated as such. Still, Castro's autonomy from Moscow notwithstanding, it is impossible to imagine Cuba's operating in Africa without Soviet consent and, in fact, massive support.

A distinction should be made between proxies and puppets. As we shall see below, the Cubans definitely have their own reasons for being in Africa. On a few occasions, they acted independently of or even contrary to Moscow's wishes (especially in Angola). Nevertheless, Castro's Africa Corps is being armed, supplied, and delivered to Africa by the Soviet Union. The fact that Havana does not blindly follow the Kremlin's dictates should be of interest in assessing Soviet–Cuban relations, but, as far as the African theater is concerned, the USSR obtained in Castro's forces an extremely convenient tool. The East German role is both more limited and more obvious. The Honnecker regime is not known to have any particular

African ambitions. Although mostly playing the Soviet game, there is also a desire to undermine or to counter West German interests.

Soviet Objectives

An assessment of Moscow's objectives in Africa is handicapped by the near absence of serious discussion in Soviet literature of the USSR's interests on that continent. The Kremlin, for public consumption, takes the position that its only desire is to do what is best for the Africans themselves. If the Kremlin is to be believed, it has no interest in African mineral riches, and neither has it a need for naval or other military facilities. Consequently, the Soviet party line suggests that if the USSR gets involved in Africa, it is strictly out of selfless generosity motivated by a moral imperative to help the national liberation, both political and economic, of newly born nations.

The Soviet record in Africa tells a different story. But to impute intentions on the basis of foreign policy activities is possible with any degree of certainty only if we first assume that we have an adequate understanding of the Soviet mindset and of the Soviet leadership's own perception of its policy steps; and second, that these steps are a product of rational planning dominated by national security considerations rather than the outcome of a complex process of bureaucratic bargaining where domestic factors, miscalculation, and inertia may play a major role.

There are probably as many lists of Soviet objectives in Africa as there are Western analysts studying them. Naval experts tend to put at the top of this list the Soviet desire for naval bases and for a capability to disrupt Western shipping. Students of Soviet foreign policy frequently give priority to Soviet rivalries with the West and with China, while scholars concerned with Soviet domestic politics emphasize the sloppiness of Moscow's policy formulation as heavily influenced by the unprecedented freedom of major bureaucratic and institutional constituencies to pursue their own ways under the aging and indecisive leadership. Those specializing in African affairs often see Soviet objectives through the prism of causes the Kremlin supports in Africa and do not share a particularly alarmist view of the USSR's motives — as long as they are not in fundamental contradiction with the African political mainstream.

The following are some basic Soviet objectives in Africa as they appear on the basis of Soviet writings, Western analyses, and extrapolations from Moscow's behavior. The list is partly speculative and not complete.

To start with, the USSR is interested in establishing a strong and irreversible presence as a major force to be reckoned with. It wants to become an accepted part of the African political terrain and to play a role in establishing parameters of local developments. Despite some impressive successes, the Soviets are less than totally confident that their long–lasting presence in Africa is firmly assured. After being expelled from a number of countries that were considered reliable friends and clients, it is going to take some time for the Kremlin to feel secure in any African nation.

Second, Moscow wants African states to develop in the general direction of the Soviet model, in the hope that they will become increasingly linked to the Soviet camp. The Kremlin publicly proclaims as its most important objective achieving the "fundamental transformation of international relations." This is expected to redefine the world order by providing a far more decisive voice to the coalition of communist and developing nations that reject "the capitalist path" and, in terms of geopolitics, are increasingly oriented toward the USSR.

Third, a reduction in Western influence is considered highly desirable. In a way, a decline in Western positions is perceived as a precondition for Soviet advances in Africa. The Soviets are deeply suspicious that the continuing involvement of most African nations in the Western–dominated international economic system cannot help but affect their political stand as well. Consequently, while Moscow is not in a position to replace the West in economic cooperation with Africa, it is consistently trying to persuade the Africans that they are being short-changed and should be more aggressive in fighting economic "neocolonialism."

Fourth, while China has not been particularly successful in Africa in recent years, the Soviets are still concerned about a lingering influence, if not the possibility of a Chinese comeback. After all, Peking maintains diplomatic relations with more than 40 African states and, like the Soviet Union, enjoys a reputation for being a patron of black liberation causes.

A recent upsurge in Chinese diplomatic activities did not

ignore Africa. A number of top–level Chinese delegations visited Africa in 1978–1979, each time making Moscow increasingly nervous. Peking's Vice Premier Li Hsien–Nien's four-nation African tour in February 1979 received Soviet media coverage disproportionate to the rather modest goals and achievements of this visit. The Kremlin surely has not overlooked a growing number of African heads of state being entertained in the Chinese capital, particularly since at least two of them — Joachim Yhombi–Opango of the Congo Republic and Samora Machel of Mozambique — are considered Soviet friends, receiving significant assistance from the USSR and its allies.

Nevertheless, one should not overestimate the importance of the Chinese factor in Soviet activities in Africa. Rivalry with Peking was not among the principal considerations behind the Soviet intervention in the African Horn. In Angola, Moscow was aware of and concerned with the Chinese connection with the National for the Total Independence of Africa (UNITA) and especially the Angolan National Liberation Front (FNLA). Nevertheless, it is likely that even without Peking's presence the combination of American and South African involvement would have provided the USSR with a pretext for displaying Cuban military muscle. In Zimbabwe the fear that the Zimbabwe National Union (ZANU), the Chinese–linked Mugabe faction, might get an upper hand if the Patriotic Front came to power in no way restrained Soviet opposition to the Muzorewa government. However, in 1979 the Soviets began to provide military support, both directly and indirectly, for ZANU. In short, the Soviet Union is concerned with the Chinese role in Africa, but Soviet foreign policy, as opposed to its rhetoric, does not show much sign of a paranoic obsession with this threat.

Fifth, by allying itself with African causes genuinely popular among the majority of developing nations, the Soviet Union wishes to position itself as a champion of Third World concerns and push the nonaligned movement closer to Moscow.

Sixth, the USSR is well aware of the great significance African raw materials have for Western economies. Here, the Soviet interest appears to be twofold: (1) to persuade African (in addition to all other resource–exporting) nations to pursue nationalization actions and to insist on higher prices; and (2) to

obtain for the Soviet Union the capability to practice a "denial strategy" in crisis situations in order to put political pressure on the West.

Finally, the Soviet military's, and in particular the navy's, interests in Africa are far more difficult to document on the basis of open Soviet sources. Nevertheless, other evidence convincingly demonstrates that the Soviet desire for naval and air facilities on the continent is indeed very real. According to official statements, the Kremlin is not seeking military bases in Africa. The fact of the matter is that though the USSR does not have bases in a traditional sense (i.e., with control and a flag over their territory), it has a number of highly usable facilities that play an important role by allowing for the growing reach of the Soviet ocean-going navy. There is a similar interest in maintaining access to important airports such as Luanda, Angola, for use in surveillance of Western naval movements. In addition to interest in developing the capability to disrupt Western sea lanes, the Soviet Union has a major interest in safeguarding the route around Africa and through the Indian Ocean, which is widely used for transportation purposes between the European and the far eastern parts of the USSR as well as for links with Soviet friends, such as Vietnam.

It is difficult to establish Soviet priorities in Africa. There is little evidence of a well–defined hierarchy of objectives. Instead, there are many indications of serious miscalculations, as well as domestic policy pressures. Whenever confronted with the necessity to make choices between incompatible goals in Africa, Soviet foreign policy begins to suffer from inconsistencies, zigzags, and immobility. In the African Horn, the Kremlin tried hard to maintain ties with Somalia, while winning over Ethiopia. Moscow overestimated its ability to control events, found itself pressured from all sides, and was eventually expelled from Somalia, thus losing its naval facilities in Berbera.

Two years earlier in Angola the Soviets initially committed themselves to the MPLA on the assumption that a left–wing Portuguese government would assure a reasonably smooth transfer of power. Instead, they found themselves in a major power play on the side of a faction heavily pressured by foreign–backed opponents. There was a real possibility of another foreign policy setback from the aftermath of missed

opportunities in Portugal and Chile. On the eve of the 25th Party Congress, the Brezhnev–dominated leadership was probably particularly anxious to come up with some spectacular international successes. Since the U.S. Congress, daunted by Vietnam, demonstrated every determination not to allow the Ford–Kissinger administration to oppose Soviet designs on the ground in Angola, and simultaneously because of the Jackson–Vanik Amendment, the Kremlin was less attracted to the potential benefits of American–Soviet cooperation. The Soviet leadership felt that foreign policy and the domestic risks of a defeat in Angola outweighed the consequences of unleashing Castro and his troops.

It appears that the Soviets were genuinely surprised by the strength of the U.S. indignation. Although Moscow was correct in predicting the American unwillingness to challenge the USSR and Cuba on the ground, it seriously miscalculated in failing to anticipate the strength of America's first post–Vietnam demonstration of disapproval of Kremlin policy — and particularly on a non–crucial issue like Angola. This does not mean, of course, that had the Soviet authorities known in advance the extent of damage the Angolan exploit would do to détente, that Moscow's performance would have been any different. Nor is there evidence to prove that the approach of the 25th Party Congress was chiefly responsible for the Politburo's abandoning its usual caution in search of foreign policy gains. One can only guess how the Kremlin would have behaved if there had been a credible threat of American counteraction, or conversely, if the Jackson–Vanik Amendment and a collapse of the U.S.–Soviet trade agreement had not already shattered the superpower rapprochement.

In summary, then, the unique circumstances of Soviet involvement in Angola and the Horn and the shortage of facts fail to indicate that the Soviets are following a coherent course based on some form of master plan to win over Africa. At the same time, the Soviet Union undoubtedly has a certain predisposition, moreover a number of unifying themes, behind its African involvement. Does this amount to strategy? Perhaps. In the final analysis, an imperfect and contradictory strategy is strategy nevertheless when it provides a general direction for foreign policy — as is happening in the case of Soviet exploits in Africa.

There are some aspects of Soviet African activities that seem to culminate in a principal unifying theme. The USSR, with great determination and consistency, works to undermine Western positions and to encourage militancy. In the case of Zimbabwe, the Kremlin takes a more extreme position than most frontline states, demanding an immediate and unconditional transfer of power to the Patriotic Front. In fact, if Soviet public statements are any reflection of its policy, Moscow would prefer that the Patriotic Front not take part in any conference with the Muzorewa government and not accept any compromise solutions. "An emerged environment in Rhodesia requires an increased vigilance and a greater sense of responsibility on the part of the Patriotic Front leadership," Moscow warned in a response to signs that peaceful settlement in Zimbabwe may be possible. With regard to Namibia, the Kremlin also coaches its South-West Africa People's Organization friends to be inflexible at the negotiating table and to rely on armed struggle.

Soviet Modus Operandi

While the Soviet Union has an almost compulsive urge to use force to prove its superpower credentials in the Third World, there seems to be a set of criteria (most likely implicit) that the Soviet leadership applies before deciding to proceed with intervention. Notwithstanding the possibility of an error in judgment that is inevitable for an emerging global power still in the process of learning the rules of the game, the Brezhnev–dominated regime has a well–deserved reputation for conservatism and pragmatism. As distasteful and threatening as Soviet actions may look to the West, Moscow's responses to the Third World (including African) targets of opportunity are calibrated and discriminating. Blind adventurism is alien to Soviet style under the tough but cautious gerontocracy.

There is also an issue of the costs of Soviet Third World exploits. Economically, Moscow's advances in the Third World do not pay off. The Kremlin as a rule has only a limited interest in gaining access to the energy and mineral resources of the developing nations. Paradoxically, the Soviets have often a more beneficial economic relationship with pro–Western states, such as Iran under the shah and Morocco, than with

their Third World allies and clients. As a matter of fact, winning over many of these nations leads to shifting the burden of economic assistance from the West to the USSR and her Eastern bloc associates. In this context the cost–conscious Soviet leadership inevitably has to think about the long–term implications of acquiring numerous demanding dependents expecting the USSR to take care of their ambitious modernization programs.

Soviet statesmen and analysts willingly admit that the arms race represents a heavy burden on their country's economic development. However, there is no discussion, at least not in public, of the price of Third World expansionism. Nevertheless, there are some grounds to believe that such discussion does take place, but it is perceived as too sensitive to be disclosed to non–elite Soviet, and especially foreign, audiences. Significantly, visiting Soviet scholars who practically never question the wisdom of the regime's international activities demonstrate an unusual independent–mindedness when Soviet aid to the Third World is involved, both military and economic. Quite a few of these semi–official Soviets go as far as expressing doubts about spending billions of rubles on the Arabs or the Africans. While Soviet economic conditions have not yet deteriorated to the degree that the leadership would seriously consider abandoning costly global ambitions, it seems reasonable that it will feel increasingly compelled to be selective in making commitments in the Third World. This selectiveness, connected with economic constraints, will have to be weighed, of course, against a growing capability to project power and a temptation to seek legitimacy in an era of domestic troubles through foreign policy successes.

Among Soviet criteria for Third World intervention, the first rule is to bet on a prospective winner or at least on a party that has a realistic chance of success. Moscow hates to waste its efforts and resources on losing causes. For such causes, it reserves, at the most, sympathetic propaganda noises and token support gestures. Second, the Kremlin does not want to find itself on the wrong side of the prevaililng mood in the Third World. This is not to suggest that the Soviet leadership always complies with the wishes of the fluid and volatile developing nations. But it is reluctant to alienate what it perceives as an important ally in its rivalry with the West by ignoring the Third

World concensus on emotional issues. Ideally, of course, Moscow desires to position itself as the standard bearer and protector of the developing nations. However, this is more a preference than a requirement. Finally, the USSR is concerned not to provoke a direct confrontation with the United States. This establishes certain limits on Soviet behavior to the degree that the Kremlin has an adequate perception of the American position and/or American determination to protect its interests with credible responses.

The Soviets as yet have been cautious about overthrowing legitimate governments in Africa. They got involved in a struggle between rival factions in Angola and conflicting governments in the Horn, but have not used dissident groups or hostile neighbors to remove pro–Western regimes. In Egypt, the Sudan, Somalia, and earlier in Ghana, the Soviet Union, despite strong displeasure, did not resist orders by local governments to withdraw its personnel. However, it is unclear what Moscow would do if it were told to leave a country where the Kremlin, in addition to advisors, technicians, and a handful of pilots, could rely on Cuban combat units. Furthermore, African governments serving as hosts to Moscow and Havana, particularly those that do not enjoy, as for instance in Ethiopia and Angola, a strong control over their population and territory, would be naturally inhibited in challenging the Kremlin by the knowledge that their very survival may depend on Soviet good graces.

Of course, needing to rely on Soviet bayonets is not a very comforting experience. As long as arms transfers, security assistance, and Cuban troops are primary Soviet exports to African nations, Moscow is unlikely to win many lasting friends or even staunch allies on the continent. Nevertheless, as unstable as the Soviet presence in Africa may be, it may shift the balance against Western interests. Even though the USSR was expelled from Egypt and Somalia, its temporary role there contributed to two major military conflicts — the Arab–Israeli war in 1973, and the Ogaden war in 1978 — both with serious damaging effects for the West. Their military presence in Angola and Ethiopia and support for the Polisario have already brought pressure on Zaire, the Sudan, and Morocco during the 1977–1979 period. The issue is not only whether the Soviets can manage to make permanent geopolitical and ideological gains in

Africa — on this score it is unlikely that their success will be as dramatic as feared by some observers — but how much damage is done in the meantime and what kind of a political landscape will be left after them. It may happen, if current trends are not arrested, that even an eventual Soviet setback will come too late for the West to capitalize upon it in full measure and will leave Africa worse off in its wake.

III. CUBAN ACTIVITES IN AFRICA*

Cuba's presence in Africa did not begin in the summer of 1975 with the military build–up in Angola. However, the scope of Havana's programs has been radically transformed from limited assistance to selected governments and revolutionary movements in the 1960s to its present large–scale involvement in Angola and Ethiopia and an expanded series of activities in a number of countries across the continent.

The current regime in Cuba has shown an interest in African affairs from the earliest days of the revolution. After the establishment of the Castro government there were contracts with revolutionary movements and "progressive" governments. Although limited in scope (never more than 1,500 advisors or troops) these activities in the early and mid–1960s demonstrated a series of policy concerns that are reflected in the decisions of the Castro government in the contemporary period. There has been a continuity in the policy decisions based on Cuban perceptions of its internationalist role and the promotion of international socialism.

Aside from medical, educational, and other assistance to African countries, Cuban military involvement has taken two basic forms: (1) the providing of military training and advisory missions, including what are in effect palace guards for regimes potentially threatened by indigenous armed forces; and (2) the providing of combat troops. Cuba began to use combat troops internationally to support friendly governments facing serious security threats in 1963, when military aid and a batallion of soldiers were sent to Algeria during the brief war with Morocco. This exercise was repeated in 1973, when 700 armored troops were sent to aid Syria in the October war. Though not a decisive factor in either conflict and despite some questions about their combat role, these troops symbolized the depth of the internationalist commitment of the Cuban government.

This internationalist duty has been reflected in the Cuban military training and advisory missions in Latin America and in the Middle East, but especially in Africa. The first Cuban military aid mission was established in Ghana in 1961. The

---

* Principal contributors to this section were Roger Fontaine and Robert Henderson.

socialist and anti–Western rhetoric of Kwame Nkrumah coincided with the anti–imperialist aspirations of Cuba. This mission remained in place until the 1966 coup against Nkrumah when it was quietly withdrawn. This coup and the 1965 coup against Ben Bella in Algeria led to a change in the size and focus of the advisory and training missions. They often became palace guards protecting certain governments against the threat of removal by indigenous military with political aspirations. The relatively low level of institutional development in many African countries made the armed forces, with their organizational, communications, and command structure and their capacity to apply overwhelming force, significant competitors for political power.

Ernesto "Che" Guevara's tour through Africa in 1964 and 1965 was not the starting point for Cuban involvement, but it was an important watershed for Cuban policy. Guevara's activities took on aspects of both the deployed combat troop and the training–advisory missions. This tour of the countries of the Casablanca Group — Algeria, Congo–Brazzaville, Dahomey, Ghana, Guinea, Tanzania, and the United Arab Republic — aimed to organize an anti–imperialist alliance based on Cuban and Algerian leadership. However, the lack of positive response by the potential member states and the minimal support of the Soviet Union, given its emphasis on peaceful coexistence with the United States and the West following the Cuban missile crisis and the debacle in the Congo, largely defused this policy initiative.

Nevertheless, Guevara in this tour established contacts and laid the groundwork for many of the policy decisions that followed in the next 10–15 years. While in Congo–Brazzaville in 1964, Guevara met with the leaderships of the various nationalist groups fighting Portuguese rule. By 1965 the MPLA, the African Party for the Independence of Guinea–Bissau and the Cape Verde Islands (PAIGC), and FRELIMO were enjoying Cuban military instruction and assistance.

In April 1965 Guevara led 200 Cuban "international fighters" in support of the secessionist movement in Congo–Leopoldville. The fighting against Moise Tshombe's government continued for 4 months in the fall of 1965 until the coup that brought Joseph Mobutu (now Mobutu Sese Seko) to power. At that point the secessionists sought an armistice with the government in

Leopoldville (now Kinshasa), and the Cubans were asked to withdraw. Guevara, disappointed in his efforts both to arrange an anti–imperialist alliance and to conduct warfare in the Congo, returned to Cuba for the effort to turn the Andes into the Sierra Maestre of Latin America. His international fighters remained in Congo–Brazzaville and Guinea, assigned to the MPLA and PAIGC training mission.

By 1966 the Cuban force in Congo–Brazzaville had grown to over 1,000 men and had trained the Civil Defense Corps, a militia organization, as a balance to the Congolese army. In June of that year, the combined efforts of the Cuban palace guard and the Civil Defense Corps crushed a military coup against the Massamba–Dabat government. However, a change in the domestic political climate eventually forced a gradual reduction of the Cuban forces to around 250 men. After the successful 1968 coup of Marien Ngouabi, the entire advisory mission was removed from the country; only a small detachment assigned to MPLA training in the south remained. Also in 1966, President Sekou Toure requested that a training and advisory mission be established in Guinea. Similar to the earlier ones in Congo–Brazzaville and Ghana, this mission has been one of the more durable, and remains in place today.

Cuba's modest presence in Africa during the 1960s contrasts sharply with the scope of the efforts today in Angola and Ethiopia. However, the motivations for activities appear to be identical. The external factor of the international environment and internal Cuban political and economic developments are the primary determinants for the policy differences between these two periods.

Differing Soviet and Cuban policy perceptions about Third World revolutionary potential in the early 1960s began to converge in the late 1960s. The period immediately following the Cuban missile crisis was a low point in Cuban–Soviet relations. Sensing the Soviets had forsaken international revolution for peaceful coexistence, Cuba sought to lessen its dependence by ending its hemispheric isolation and promoting Latin American revolution, in the hopes that compatible regimes would come to power. Simultaneously, it sought to promote an alliance of smaller socialist powers to combat imperialism and to help North Vietnam by distracting the United States with "one, two, many Vietnams," in Latin America.

This active internationalist policy reflected both Cuban insecurity about U.S. intentions given its willingness to use its military thousands of miles from home and a distrust of the Soviet pursuit of peaceful coexistence in the face of U.S. aggression in South Vietnam. Cuba feared that it might be a victim of U.S. aggression, and the Soviets might not help in its defense.

Cuban support for the Czechoslovakian invasion by the Warsaw Pact is seen by many observers as the transitional event marking the beginning of a Soviet and Cuban convergence of perceptions in international affairs. The 1970–1972 period saw a gradual re–emergence of Cuba from the domestic economic turmoil that coincided with the realization of America's defeat in South Vietnam. A Soviet and Cuban reappraisal of revolutionary opportunities in the Third World began, as the Cuban perception of an American threat receded.

Escalation in Africa: The Motives

The Cubans moved into Angola beginning in the summer of 1975 with a swiftness that stunned the Western world. Although not completely known, the reasons for Havana's decision can be divided into two sets: those internal and those external to Cuba.

Internally, there were at least four factors that positively influenced Castro's decision to enter Angola in 1975. First, the campaign to export revolution throughout Latin America had met increasingly effective resistance. Guevara's death in Bolivia simply reinforced what had been made clear earlier in Guatemala, Peru, and Venezuela, and elsewhere. The rhetoric continued, but by mid–1972 Castro himself explicitly changed his views on Latin America and its revolutionary potential. Cuba's commander–in–chief became more tolerant of the region's regimes, and Cuba's efforts at subversion were suitably scaled down. The need for revolutionary expansion was temporarily bottled up and the availability of non–regional activities satisfied the need to express the revolutionary ardor.

Second, by the mid–1970s, Cuba had begun to recover from the worst effects of the unsuccessful effort in 1970 to expand its sugar harvest by 10 million tons in that seriously dislocated and already fragile economy. The Cuban leadership devoted con-

siderable attention to this recovery and by 1973 the economic situation had improved to the extent that the Cuban government turned to other things than simply economic survival.

Third, Cuba's military has markedly improved since the revolution. By the early 1970s it no longer resembled the old rebel army in training, tactics, or equipment. In the context of the Third World, the Cuban army had become a powerful conventional force, equipped with sophisticated Soviet arms. However, the new Cuban armed forces became an organization without a clear mission. Designed originally as a home defense force, its capabilities far exceeded the need — a need rendered moot in any case because of the tacit acceptance by the United States of the permanence of the Cuban regime.

Fourth, Castro has never been content to play a small role in history — either Cuba's or the world's. His ambitions have remained great. In retrospect, there was little reason for the view commonly held in the early 1970s that Castro had diminished his personal desires to play a role beyond Cuba.

These four factors, then, were in place in late 1974 and early 1975 when the opportunities for an expansion of Cuba's foreign policy horizons arose.

The formulation of Cuban foreign policy is as complex and as dependent on external factors as that of other states. The decision to risk considerable prestige in a large–scale intervention in Angola in late October and early November 1975, was not taken lightly by the Cuban leadership. It reflected a variety of motivations, some in conflict with others. The external factors fall under four general headings: the Angolan milieu, African international political considerations, and the U.S. reaction and the Soviet role.

The Angolan Milieu. The Cuban intervention in Angola must be put into perspective against previous Cuban military and assistance efforts in Africa. Ideologically compatible regimes and political movements had received amounts of aid and assistance that were dwarfed by the Cuban effort in Angola. While there were important precedents based on ideological compatibility, the quantities of personnel and materiel were something new.

The collapse of Portuguese authority in its African territories after the April 1974 revolution was the immediate change in climate that prompted Havana. Cuban military personnel ar-

rived in small but growing numbers before the final pull–out of the Portuguese in November 1975.

African International Politics. Cuba has been very careful to enter and expand its African operations only on invitation from African leaders. Additionally, the Cubans realized their armed forces could be highly effective on a continent dotted with unstable governments and low–quality security forces. Angola was an ideal first choice because there was no established authority with which to contend.

The Cubans were presented, however, with a dangerous foe in South Africa. That country's actions in support of UNITA triggered, according to Castro, Cuban intervention on behalf of the MPLA. Havana's chronology of action and reaction is highly questionable, but the use of South Africa as the principal enemy provided the Cubans with a solid rationale for action. Politically, this became its greatest advantage before black African audiences. This sense of moral legitimacy is likely to be an important factor encouraging Castro to want to be involved in the continuing southern African problems.

The U.S. Reaction. Another key factor was the presumption of a passive reaction from Cuba's principal adversary, the United States. In 1975 this country was in no mood to check a Cuban thrust into Africa. Castro, an excellent interpreter of American moods, took full advantage of the opportunity in as prudent (that is, secretive) a manner as possible.

The Soviet Role. The role of the Soviet Union is the last external influence, quite possibly the most important, and is the most difficult with which to deal. In this relationship, Cuba has been characterized as being either a partner or a pawn. If the Soviets simply dictated Cuban participation, then Havana's motives are hardly worth examining. However, the evidence indicates that the reality of Cuban involvement in Africa is not that simple.

Cuba's role in Africa must first be considered an expression of its leaders' world view, that is buttressing Havana's self–imposed revolutionary duty. There has been a constant confluence of Soviet and Cuban interests in each of the Cuban activities. In this light, the Angolan effort reflected a shared concern with a positive outcome. In Ethiopia, however, although the Ogaden action was similar to Angola, the war in Eritrea (in which Cuban advisors have been killed by former

clients, the Eritrean People's Liberation Front and ELF) can be seen as having the potential to create tension between the Soviet Union and Cuba, though evidence of that has yet to surface.

There has been an evolution in Castro's thinking on approaches to the promotion of revolution during the 1960s and 1970s. From 1960 to 1965 the Cubans worked against entrenched, conservative regimes throughout Latin America. The goal of turning the Andes into the Sierre Maestre of Latin America was never reached. The staying power of the governments and the revolutionary potential of the Latin American masses were both misconstrued. In the 1970s, targets for Cuban foreign activity were more carefully selected and when possible Havana worked with existing governments or established political movements. This expanded capacity to work with established organizations marked an important evolutionary step in the Cuban operating style. Moreover, in contrast to the Latin American effort, the Cuban military engagements in Africa were based on the application of overwhelming logistical support and concentrations of firepower reflecting the indirect but heavy involvement of the Soviet Union.

Cuba vigorously denies its being forced to do anything by the Soviet Union. Carlos Rafael Rodrigues, the third ranking member of the Cuban politburo, has pointed out that the decision to go into Angola was Cuba's; after all, the first contingents from the island were transported by Cuban ships and planes. While it is unlikely the Soviets played no role at all at the beginning, as Rodrigues suggests, it is likely the Cubans moved in at their own risk while Moscow cautiously monitored the American reaction.

Key Constraints on Activities

For a small power, Cuba operates in Africa with a remarkable lack of constraint, either domestic or foreign. However, there are a few inhibiting factors and there are likely to be more in the future. Of these constraints, no doubt the most important in the long run are domestic. They are also the least understood and least susceptible to precise measurement.

Cuba carefully monitors domestic discontent. There are hints that Cuban public opinion is having some effect on Havana's

African policy. Limited evidence suggests that the African ventures are not universally popular. Managers complain about the drain of skilled manpower in military service, which the still fragile Cuban economy can ill afford, and ordinary Cubans believe shortages (especially food) are the result of Cuba's presence in Angola and Ethiopia.

The official response to this minimal discontent has been twofold. First in 1977 and part of 1978, Castro made speeches throughout the island having a common theme: The Cuban people never had it so good. Second, in order to entice volunteers for African assignments, special privileges are given, including television sets and priority treatment on housing requests. Castro recently chastized an audience in Havana, saying that people were eager to serve in Africa but lethargic in their efforts to strengthen the revolution in Cuba through increased production.

Complaints about casualties are more harshly dealt with than complaints about economic conditions, and consequently less is heard about that subject in Cuba. Nevertheless, coping with domestic unease may become the most serious internal problem faced by the regime since the early 1960s. Indeed, it may be the reason for a few conciliatory statements made by Castro and his foreign minister Isidoro Malmierca on Zimbabwe and Namibia. In any case, Cuba has never participated at this level in a foreign war until now, and its long–term impact can only be speculated. It is likely that more attention will be paid domestic feelings than in the past. It is not clear, however, that such attention would act as a brake to more expanded commitments, should the opportunity arise.

It is important to examine organizational interests when analyzing popularity and potential for long–term commitments to a given government's policy. It is now reasonably certain that the bureaucrats — at least the younger, better trained ones — in the economic ministries are the least supportive of the regime's African wars for a number of sound reasons. The first is that these foreign activities have drawn government attention and resources away from their primary areas of responsibility — economic development, education, health services, etc. Another consideration is institutional jealousy. Promotion and advancement in the military are accelerated as the military organization grows. Prestige and resources are di-

rected into the expansion of that bureaucracy over the other competing bureaucracies. For example, two of the five vice presidents appointed to the new Council of State in 1976 were division generals, Senan Casas and Abelardo Colome, who had served with distinction in Angola. But economic managers in the Cuban bureaucracy are unlikely to risk careers by criticizing foreign policy decisions at this time. They may, however, eventually press for more economic development, but this factor should be watched and interpreted carefully. Dissent may come in the form of warnings about serious discontent as the economy continues to stagnate despite increasing Soviet aid.

There are four types of foreign constraints on Cuban activities in Africa. The first is provided by their reliance on Soviet material and logistics for their expeditionary force. Although the Cubans initially transported their troops to Angola in converted freighters and in their own aircraft, they could not stage a massive infusion of troops similar to the late December 1975 and January 1976 Angolan effort or the winter 1977–1978 surge in Ethiopia without the Soviet Union. It is doubtful that the Cubans could operate on a major scale anywhere in Africa if such operations jeopardized Soviet interests. Thus far, their joint activities have shown close cooperation and coordination, with only rare exceptions.

A second constraint would be a stronger negative reaction from the United States to Cuban activity. So far, the United States has done little to restrain the Cubans effectively. The serious warnings issued by Kissinger in 1976 that no further Angolas would be tolerated were not taken seriously in Havana. The success of the Cuban effort in the Horn of Africa has solidified this sense of U.S. impotence in short–term security matters, at least in this area of the Third World.

A third constraint is the Republic of South Africa. The Cubans have had mixed results militarily in direct combat with South Africans or South African–led troops. Engagements in Angola in 1975 caused the South Africans to reconsider their tactical doctrine and upgrade their mobile artillery and armor capabilities. Cubans suffered minor setbacks in the early days of the Angola operation against the South Africans, but the South African withdrawal led to quick victories against the FNLA and UNITA. Still, a determined South African defense of Namibia or other southern African targets — a defense that

would not rule out other Cassinga–style raids — would have a most sobering effect in Havana.

The final constraint is a negative African reaction and the willingness of other international actors to support that reaction. This was best demonstrated by the support for the Mobutu regime by Morocco, Senegal, Belgium, France, and others during the invasion of Shaba province by Katangese staging out of Angola. This type of constraint could be imposed on the Cubans by moderate African powers, but cooperation among these states has been unpredictable and would have to coincide with circumstances that engage Western interests.

Nevertheless, African political sensitivites provide the most effective constraint on Cuban military activity in the contemporary period. Cuba has been able to operate against white regimes (Rhodesia) or in a civil war where the opposition was supported by a white regime (Angola). It also has been able to support regimes facing an invasion (Ethiopia from Somalia). The OAU aversion to cross–border attacks on sovereign governments has not, however, been softened in the wake of the Tanzanian invasion of Uganda. Even those African countries that supported the Cuban effort in Angola have begun to show concern at signs that there are no indications of a reduction in their presence.

Future Developments

Havana's foreign policy interests are not confined to Africa. Its interest in promoting revolution in South America, for example, is still very much alive. Its tactics and perceived opportunities may have changed, but the objective has not. Moreover, tactics and opportunities may well change again in the region as is the case currently in Nicaragua where Havana has actively supported the Sandinistas with more than propaganda support. However, Havana's activist foreign policy must be put back into a wider context than the African continent to establish the correct perspective.

Cuba is not a large country. Its resources and manpower have been strained by the overseas commitments to Latin America, South Yemen, and Africa. Any major expansion in effort would be difficult at this time.

Angola in a sense was a testing ground. An early disaster in

late 1975 in that country would have controlled Havana's appetite for further adventure. However, Angola and Ethiopia have served as a domestically and, in some cases, internationally popular demonstration of Cuba's new weight in world affairs. They have been effective as springboards for more activity in central and southern Africa, with particular attention to Namibia and Zaire.

To a remarkable degree, Cuba's current interests in Africa are devoid of economic advantage. Castro has repeatedly stated that Cuba does not "have a single bank, a single hectare of land, a mine, an oil well or a factory — absolutely nothing," in Africa. Cuba does, however, have its fishing fleet working the rich waters off the Angolan coast. Nevertheless, after 4 years of heavy involvement in Africa, Cuba has not reaped any important economic advantages directly from Africa.

Cuba has played well its role in Africa in terms of not offending black African sensibilities. Havana cannot disregard its Moscow connection, but the emphasis has been put on the other, more "legitimate" reasons in the African perspective — socialist solidarity support for liberation movements, internationalist duty, war against racism, etc. — for Cuba's African activities. Moreover, Havana has actively advanced its position within the nonaligned movement and has continued to pursue the goal of an anti-imperialist alliance. However, this effort has come under heavy criticism from a number of nonaligned countries who believe that Soviet hegemony is as great a threat as U.S. imperialism. Within the OAU, Nigerian Head of State Olusegun Obasanjo openly challenged those who would provide military assistance from the outside to African countries by underscoring the importance of African invitations to those outsiders and by cautioning against overstaying welcomes once the immediate security problems have been resolved.

There are several factors that could increase Cuban difficulty in Africa and the international arena as a whole.

First would be a Cuban military defeat. If the Cubans were to prove vulnerable, African respect and support would decrease quite rapidly.

Second, strong support by the United States for those African and other critics of Cuba would encourage them to continue their campaign of criticism of Cuba within the nonaligned movement and the OAU. At the Belgrade Meeting of the Non-

aligned Movement, President Josip Tito himself spoke out vociferously against Cuban activities in Africa. He was joined by several other leaders from a variety of geographic perspectives. A number of other countries have been critical of Cuba's lingering presence on the continent, especially as a sign of Soviet presence there.

Third, Havana's difficulties would increase if it violated its own ground rules and those of the OAU. If Cuban forces directly and openly participated in an invasion of an independent black state — such as Zaire or Somalia — serious political criticisms would arise. Simultaneously, Cuban aspirations for leadership within the nonaligned movement would be brought into question.

Fourth, Cuba's credibility would be damaged if its actions were seen as a mere function of Soviet ambitions. Although international and particularly Third World criticism of this sort has become more prevalent, the Cuban leadership will remain vigilant in the protection of their international image. Events in Eritrea have the potential to seriously erode this effort. But thus far the Cuban role has been an advisory and logistical one rather than a direct combat one. In addition, there is some evidence that the Soviet ambivilance and Cuban constancy regarding the Neto regime have created minor stresses in their relationship. This situation became apparent following an unsuccessful coup against Neto by a pro–Soviet faction within the MPLA in April 1977. The Cubans participated in crushing the effort to unseat Neto, and publicly endorsed Neto's regime; Moscow, though forewarned of the effort, remained silent on the whole affair.

There are vulnerable points that can be exploited in the Soviet–Cuban alliance in their African activity. The greatest opportunity will be provided by the growing inability of Havana to spell out for itself a clearly independent role — that is, a policy that in the future does more than serve the immediate African interests of the Soviet Union. That problem will be compounded should there be a lengthening list of Cuban casualties that in turn will mean an increase in the domestic tension over involvement in Africa. The Cuban perception that it is doing more than its fair share will also increase to the extent that Cubans will be called upon to bear the brunt of the fighting in any future conflict in Angola, Somalia, Zimbabwe, or South

Africa. Finally, Cuban discomfort will increase in direct proportion to the amount of criticism it receives within the nonaligned movement.

Does Cuba have a grand design? It surely has short–term goals and tactics for achieving them, perhaps even an overall strategy for operating in the Third World. Havana sees itself as the cutting edge of a revolution wholly incompatible with American capitalism and supportive of Soviet goals for global socialism. The Cuban leaders see themselves as a bridge between the Third World and Moscow. They also relish being Peking's most trenchant critic in the Third World. This in itself does not constitute a grand design, but Havana does display a sense of its place in the world and its role in history. More likely, the tension of being Moscow's cat's–paw in Africa and attempting not to appear so will continue. The political justifications for military involvement will continue to hinge on effectively conforming to African political expectations.

IV. SUGGESTIONS FOR U.S. POLICY

It is not a question of whether to ignore Africa's current turmoil or to plunge into it, reflexively responding to each Soviet–Cuban thrust. A balance must be struck between measures aimed at the external (communist) dimension of the problem and the indigenous African one. The number of African governments proclaiming adherence to Marxist or scientific socialist principles is of far less importance than their motivations for doing so. On the other hand, there is no basis for assuming that the superficiality of ideological stances in the 1960–1974 period applies today. The facts of power and dependence have changed, and a new set of relations is in the process of development, whose outcome will reflect, in part, the participation of external powers.

Assuming that Western interests are at stake during the current period of change, opinions nonetheless differ widely as to the importance of those interests and the best means of advancing them. While these debates cannot be finally resolved here, three general observations are pertinent to the policy-making community. First, some degree of congruence and consistency is required in developing the various aspects of an African policy. A high level of rhetoric and diplomatic energy will achieve little, and perhaps prove counterproductive, if not accompanied by real policy resources including political commitment to stances taken, and economic and military aid. The risks in overstating what the United States is actually prepared to do are underscored by the salience of insecurity and dependence in contemporary Africa.

On the other hand, a relatively high level of policy commitment to Africa is not sustainable unless it is based on public understanding and support. The combination of domestic apathy and polarized emotions on African issues must itself be addressed before a significantly higher level of effort in Africa is possible. The evidence of recent years suggests that it may not be possible to formulate effective policies by relying primarily on domestically "safe" postures or on the search for "high ground," which avoids domestic controversy. Yet, there will be few alternatives unless policy makers are prepared to frame their proposals and decisions in terms that make sense to a broader range of domestic groups.

Washington is thus confronted with both a short–term and a longer–term problem. Some would argue that it is simply not possible for the Executive Branch, in the current domestic and international climate, to find the "right" formula for attracting domestic support for an activist policy. The congressional mood, in particular, may not lend itself to any "quick fix" in African policy. Washington may be stuck with a policy that is buffeted between the emotions of "race war" and "cold war" until such time as events in Africa or a new administration in Washington permits a fresh look at policy assumptions. Policy makers, however, have an obligation to identify the tangible costs of an effective policy as well as the costs of continuing on the current course. Over the longer term, there is no reason to assume that today's disorders are a passing phenomenon. Whether or not Washington decides that a greater level of effort is required in Africa, the need for congruence and consistency will continue.

Second, the U.S. interests at stake in Africa are of a lower order than European interests there, but this does not make them any less real. The interests of our European allies are neither an "obstacle" to U.S. policy nor a mere colonial legacy without risks to overall allied relationships. Europe's ties in Africa reflect history, geography, and a natural interdependence that is as real today as it was during the colonial period. The forms of European–African association, such as the Lomé Convention on trade and development assistance, are based on common interests freely negotiated. For African states, the European connection is their most important external economic linkage.

While the role of Africa in European trade and investment has declined since the 1960s, it has increased in absolute terms and is considerably higher than Africa's role in U.S. trade and investment. Similarly, European (and Japanese) reliance on African raw materials far outstrips that of the United States, and such reliance continues to grow. This pattern of economic links applies across the black–white divide in southern Africa and includes those industrial allies that were not colonial powers as well as those that were. While the French (and to a much lesser extent the Belgians) are at present the only Europeans prepared to become involved in Africa's politico–military problems in a direct way, a number of European governments have

voiced their concern at the recent drift of events in Africa, including the Germans and the new Thatcher government in the United Kingdom. In sum, the facts of geography and long-established trade routes and economic ties assure that African problems have a greater salience and immediacy to Europeans than to Americans. A failure to reflect such realities in U.S. policy could cause continuing strains and divisions in the Western approach to African issues, and reduce possibilities for effective Western collaboration.

Given the complex interplay of African, European, and global interests at stake for the United States, some effort must be made to address each aspect of the situation. It may be that the most appropriate way to address Soviet–Cuban behavior in Africa is not by Western counter–intervention, but by global policy measures aimed at restraining or opposing such activity more generally. The U.S. initiative leading to talks with the Soviets about conventional arms transfers to the Third World are one positive type of measure that deserves continued support. However, it is necessary to recognize that the United States has limited carrots with which to induce Soviet restraint in Africa. Without getting mired in past debates about "linkage," it is clear that overall U.S.–Soviet relations are conditioned by specific events and regional trends. The relationship of the Indian Ocean naval limitation talks to events in the Horn of Africa are only one example of how the process can work.

Rather than back away from discussion of such relationships, it may be more useful to be quite specific about them in both public and diplomatic channels. There are U.S.–African reasons as well as U.S.–Soviet reasons for concern, and these must somehow be reflected in policy. It is difficult to see how U.S. interests in racial accommodation, expanded market and resource access, and improved standards of human welfare can be advanced by taking a back seat in Africa whenever its tensions explode into conflict. By the same token, U.S. interests will suffer if the doctrine of African solutions to African problems is translated to mean that American policy will back whatever changes emerge on the ground without U.S. participation.

To the extent that the United States perceives a need to take action and to respond in Africa, such activity should not be purely reative to Soviet–Cuban moves. There are probably a

limited number of African situations in which a direct U.S. role would be feasible. Washington needs a strategy, not merely a set of instincts, if it is to gain momentum and initiative of its own. Furthermore, there is evidence in past actions by Moscow and Havana to suggest that they select their opportunities with some care, with a view not only to African sentiment but also to the feasibility of a direct Western response. Consequently, greater attention needs to be paid to the context of conflict and the nature of bilateral relations so that American purposes have some chance of being realized.

Third, it does not suffice to argue that the United States and its industrial allies can accommodate major political change on the continent. The direction and nature of such change depends on who participates in it, and is not predetermined by historical forces, except at the crudest level of analysis. More important, the transitional process now under way could be prolonged, opening up the prospect of a continuous deterioration of conditions and growing damage to Western interests. This is especially pertinent in the economic and resource field where it may not be the end result of change that hampers Western interests, but the process of change. In sum, it matters not only where Africa is going but how it gets there.

The Instruments of Policy

The relationship among security, development, and human welfare is as complex in Africa as in other regions. Policy measures aimed at addressing Soviet–Cuban activity should be based upon an awareness that the continent has specific problems and circumstances that make it highly vulnerable to external influences. As indicated earlier, such vulnerability takes political, economic, and military forms but is essentially a problem of institutional weakness. Small increments of money and arms can prove to be highly disruptive of domestic and regional stability, transport routes, exports, and development plans. Putting institutions back together again often proves far more difficult than damaging them. Similarly, it is important to recognize that Africa consists not only of nationalist and egalitarian ideologies and aspirations for development, but also of individual states, governments, and leaders whose first priority must be survival. While the ingredients of survival vary

from state to state, a sense of security, in all its dimensions, ranks high on the list and can be considered the precondition for development and expanded human welfare.

The implications of this analysis are twofold. First, the effectiveness of Western policies will vary directly with the resources supporting them. While Africans demand that outsiders align themselves on the "right" side of issues such as majority rule and respect for national sovereignty, a wide range of possibilities exists for implementing such alignment. Moreover, the impact of external policies is not necessarily dependent on the extent to which they are, or are seen to be, "pro–African" on the level of general principles. In fact, the concept of being pro–African is increasingly ambiguous in a period when Africans are fighting each other in growing numbers. The extent of recent Soviet gains in southern Africa and Ethiopia reflects above all the commitment of tangible resources.

Second, to the extent that the industrial democracies share some common interests in Africa, it must be recognized that some coordination of effort is called for. This applies in the formulation of policy toward the transitions to majority rule, but also in the provision of aid resources, the maintenance of political and diplomatic support for friendly governments, and the adoption of public postures toward the issue of Soviet–Cuban activity. Such coordination need not be deterred by predictable accusations from various sources that the West is "ganging up" on Africa, any more than the Soviets and their allies are so deterred.

Among the vehicles that could be used to a greater extent for collaborative purposes are ad hoc, one–country planning groups; development–oriented regional instruments such as the Club du Sahel; existing African bodies such as the African Development Bank; and OECD and North Atlantic Treaty Organization fora (where appropriate). It may be that new vehicles of coordination are needed and could be developed along informal lines, much as the Western Five concept in Namibia emerged at U.S. initiative.

To be sure, there are diverging as well as converging U.S. and allied interests in Africa, which no amount of "coordination" can disguise. There is also an element of commercial and resource competition inherent in the U.S.–allied relationship in Africa. But the current lack of joint effort is the product of an

earlier time when African issues were less important to us and our allies (except perhaps Britain and France). To continue with only sporadic and faint–hearted efforts to deal jointly in Africa may be a luxury in the current period.

Some specific choices can now be outlined. If it is determined that the United States does indeed have major (if not vital) interests in Africa, the time has perhaps come for more explicit public recognition of the need to back those interests in meaningful ways. To date, the interests identified by official sources and political leaders are described in almost self–executing terms: We wish to have friendly relations with African states because of our growing interest in African markets and resources; we become involved in the search for settlements in southern Africa because of our interest in peaceful change and majority rule. Absent from the discussion is any recognition of the possible political, economic, and even military costs of advancing such interests.

Among the actions that should be seriously pursued, assuming that U.S. interests are becoming more important, are: increased arms sales ceilings and military training; greater use of politically motivated economic aid (sometimes inappropriately called "security supporting assistance") on a flexible basis to strengthen selected governments; the launching with our industrial allies of a major economic assistance initiative for Africa; increased manpower development programming for Africa; official sponsorship of a series of government–business dialogues to explore obstacles to (and opportunities for) expanded U.S. private economic involvement in African development; meaningful aid to southern African refugees; expanded programs of training, especially in civil administration; the buttressing of free and independent labor organizations; and some support for the development of political party structures.

The focus and objective of such efforts would require careful elaboration. In the economic field, U.S. and Western efforts would concentrate on economic and administrative stabilization and the creation of an environment conducive to expanded private investment. Other thrusts might include expanding African food output and strengthening African training and educational institutions. This approach should not imply reduced U.S. participation in international lending institutions;

but it would signify that Western nations are prepared to launch their own programs on a substantial scale, to overcome long–standing rivalries and divisions among the industrial allies in Africa, and to avoid becoming enmeshed in the politicized and often polemical debates over economic cooperation in various New International Economic Order fora.

If, indeed, it is easier to destroy than to build institutions, the implication for U.S. policy is that greater emphasis be given to supporting the capacity to govern. Civilian institutions are an important dimension of political development, as non–governmental efforts in the field of education and organized labor have long realized. U.S. policy must recognize Africa's need for stronger, more durable, and less easily politicized institutions. If the Soviet role in Africa has a narrowly military thrust when compared to that of the United States, this implies that greater effort is needed to coordinate the various dimensions of a U.S. presence in African countries. Among the criteria that should influence U.S. choices in bilateral diplomacy in Africa are: a government's past and current attitude on issues of direct importance to the United States, both regionally and globally; its attitude to foreign investment; its posture on superpower competition and its readiness to support measures, including regional peace–keeping efforts aimed at checking Soviet influence; and the inherent economic and geopolitical importance of the state itself.

In the security field, expanded U.S. involvement would take the form of strengthening the security forces of selected friendly governments, including those living amidst ongoing regional tensions. Four thrusts of policy would be pursued. First, Washington could initiate discussions with key allies with a view to encouraging their continued and, if possible, expanded role in providing equipment and training to appropriate African recipients.

Second, Washingtion would identify two or three important African states whose security forces might be appropriate candidates for strengthening and support, looking toward their possible participation in future inter–African or Western–African peace–keeping operations. Existing purchasers of U.S. military equipment such as Kenya, the Sudan, and Morocco could be on this list, but Nigeria would also be encouraged to join it.

Third, Washington (with British cooperation if possible) would expand its modest new sales and training program for Botswana, and extend it to Zambia as well. The explicit purpose would be to show Western interest in the security problems of these countries, and to provide a margin of superiority for these forces over those of resident guerrilla groups and armed refugees. Similarly, Washington would stand ready to support the embryonic forces of Namibia if the circumstances of the transition to independence would permit. The option of providing security assistance for Mozambique and other Marxist governments should be available if there are foreign policy reasons to do so. Programs to train and support civilian police units should be instituted.

Fourth would be to give active encouragement to the OAU to develop a meaningful peace–keeping force. After years of failing to take such a force seriously, the OAU summit in Monrovia in July 1979 gave the idea of such a force support for the first time. Although unlikely in the short term, this force could serve both African and U.S. security interests in a wide variety of uses. Accordingly, it may be appropriate to signal formally to selected, friendly governments a U.S. willingness to offer advice, training, and possibly materiel support for OAU peace–keeping purposes. The advent to the OAU chairmanship of President William Tolbert of Liberia — who has specifically called for the OAU to develop its capacity in this field — may offer an opportunity for such an initiative. While the obstacles to effective OAU defense collaboration are both political and military, the United States should be prepared to signal its willingness to help with some of the major tangible military elements, such as training and logistics.

A related option to be considered is a program of gradually expanded U.S. naval visits and presence in African waters. The purpose of such a program would be to signal Western interest in African issues, while providing a basis for demonstrating U.S. concern in crisis situations. The signal to Moscow would be that it can no longer assume an absence of Western naval power in the region and an uncontested capability to be first on the scene, with all this implies in the context of crisis diplomacy. Renewed U.S. use of South African military and naval facilities would be out of the question in the absence of significant political change. However, Washington may want to consider devel-

oping the means for at least an intermittent naval presence in southern African waters so as to project an independent capability (independent, that is, of South Africa) to operate in the area.

Global Actions

The Soviet–Cuban alliance was not formed in Africa, and there is no reason to think it can be ended there. Hence, it may be more realistic to conceive U.S. policy toward Soviet–Cuban ties in the broader context of U.S.–Soviet and U.S.–Cuban relations. Nonetheless, in Africa our objective should be to hamper Soviet–Cuban operations, to raise their price, to find meaningful ways to respond, or to deter them altogether. Since Soviet policy in Africa today is heavily dependent on the Cuban factor, ways to limit that factor should be found, thus limiting Soviet freedom of action. Although this is not easily done, there are some ways.

One set of U.S.–Cuban measures that must be raised is the issue of our bilateral diplomatic, economic, and cultural relationship. The current stance is inconsistent. If we are not even prepared to threaten the mini–rapprochement of the past 2 years with Havana, why should Havana take us seriously on African issues? There is no basis for assuming that the United States can effectively isolate its bilateral relationship with Cuba from its stance toward the Cubans in Africa. Accordingly, if we wish to oppose the latter more directly, consideration should be given to reviewing the basis for the recent rapprochement. A wide range of steps can be envisaged to signal our African concerns, depending on specific circumstances in Africa. Steps could include breaking off existing discussions on bilateral issues, downgrading the U.S. presence, expelling Cuban personnel in the United States, stepping up surveillance of Cuban military movements, developing more active information programming on Cuba's African activities, and the like.

It will not be possible in the foreseeable future for the United States to reach an understanding with Castro's Cuba. One high priority area is Cuba's vulnerability to major attack — by the United States and others, including China — an attack to undermine the Cuban desire to be a leader of the nonaligned nations. In the future, active diplomacy in nonaligned capitals

should be aimed at making nonalignment an honest concept, thus discrediting Cuba. Much of this diplomacy should be aimed at encouraging open criticism by Africans of Cuba's nonaligned credentials.

Another set of measures would take place in Africa itself: to try to raise the on–the–ground price for Cuba via propaganda efforts, aid to neighboring governments that oppose Cuban efforts, and political support for third parties that are doing these things.

Our overall stance vis–à–vis Zimbabwe, Namibia, and South Africa is obviously central to the character of our African policy. If the United States makes clear that South African or Zimbabwean recalcitrance and cross–border strikes justify further measures against them under Chapter VII, it is inviting additional Cuban involvement in these conflicts. The United States does not have to praise the actions of white–ruled states in order to avoid legitimizing Cuban activity. At the least, U.S. policy should contain some elements of ambiguity as to potential future actions so as to avoid legitimizing in advance either Cuban or South African policy.

On the other hand, Western policy will run aground if the West acts (or fails to act) in ways that suggest tacit or overt alignment with Pretoria. Under the new conditions of an African–led government in Salisbury, U.S. moves suggesting a more sympathetic approach — if taken — should be accompanied by moves indicating a more active American policy throughout the region and a greater readiness to compete with Moscow. It is difficult to see how Washington can compete in the current climate if it divides African governments artifically into "good" ones and "bad" ones and refuses to deal at all with key actors in the region. In the case of Angola, this would simply confirm that country's existing pattern of dependence and alignment. The Western goal, presumably, is to offer alternatives to both communist–and South African–orchestrated solutions in southern Africa.

Looked at structurally, the Soviet–Cuban military activity is comparable to the 1978 Western–African operation in Zaire. The United States should make clear its readiness to respond similarly again if necessary but should indicate its preference for UN or OAU operations to avoid polarizing African conflicts. This would place more political onus on Moscow and Havana for

polarizing in the first place, while justifying future Western efforts.

The United States does not have the power or credibility to coerce Havana into backing down by veiled threats of naval action or intervention against Cuba itself. More credible would be to focus on Cuba's logistic and supply dependence on Moscow and to threaten one or more forms of linkage (not SALT necessarily) in the U.S.–Soviet context.

Since from the Soviet standpoint, their involvement in Africa is an integral part of the overall historic rivalry with the West and particularly with the United States, the issue often will have to be approached on a global level. If the Soviets move a pawn in Africa, the West may be wise to move a queen in some completely different area or plateau of the relationship. For this, developing better instrumentalities for affecting Soviet behavior is of crucial importance. The United States today is increasingly viewed by Moscow as a hostile, but simultaneously indecisive power. Congressional constraints on credible responses to Soviet expansion, coupled with artificial barriers to the development of trade with the USSR, leave the Executive Branch few incentives and penalties to ensure American positions being perceived as very relevant by the Kremlin. It is imperative for any U.S. administration to have greater freedom of action, both in competing and in cooperating with a formidable Soviet rival.

If pre–emption attempts do not succeed, the United States may wish to encourage opposition to Soviet exploits on the part of African nations toward whom the Kremlin appears to be sensitive. It can also be demonstrated to the Soviets, as in Zaire, that some African states are prepared to counter cross–border adventures that depend on Soviet hardware and Soviet clients, and that they will receive Western support in doing so. The purpose will be to upgrade the competition and make it more costly and risky for Moscow at selected points. It may in some cases be desirable to consider the use of Western proxies and covert activity to help stiffen African forces that cannot count on support from other friendly sources. Soviet air– and sealift capabilities, in the absence of their having a major, permanent presence in the Indian and south Atlantic oceans, are dependent upon at least the tacit cooperation of a number of nations, including American allies such as Turkey. Every pos-

sible effort should be made to deny the Soviets overflight and refueling privileges during conflict situations.

All these measures, even if implemented efficiently and in a coherent fashion, are not a panacea. The best they can achieve is a narrowing of opportunities for Soviet military engagement in Africa, making such an engagement less attractive due to the costs and risks attached. The more productive course of action, discussed above, is to be interested, willing, and able to help African states solve their problems.

Finally, it is important to develop a general unifying theme for U.S. foreign policy to demonstrate that, after its post–Vietnam, post–Watergate soul–searching, America is more mature and more determined. The United States must be more determined to stand up for what are considered really essential national interests, but mature enough to be aware of the limits of U.S. power and the complexities of the modern world, including the African arena.

V. APPENDIX

***

A. Bolaji Akinyemi
Nigerian Institute of International Affairs

David Albright
Problems of Communism

Major General Anderson W. Atkinson
Defense Attache System

Pauline Baker
Senate Foreign Relations Committee

Gerald J. Bender
University of Southern California at Los Angeles

Gordon R. Beyer
Bureau of African Affairs
Department of State

Henry Bienen
Princeton University

Johnnetta Cole
University of Massachusetts

L. Gray Cowan
State University of New York at Albany

Chester A. Crocker
Center for Strategic and International Studies

Roger W. Fontaine
Center for Strategic and International Studies

Brigadier General Billy Forsman
Current Intelligence
Defense Intelligence Agency

Irving Louis Horowitz
Rutgers University

Robert G. Houdek
Bureau of African Affairs
Department of State

E. Brian Latell
Georgetown University, and National Foreign Assessment
  Center, Central Intelligence Agency

Robert Legvold
Council on Foreign Relations

William LeoGrande
American University

Rear Admiral James Lyons
Joint Chiefs of Staff

David E. McGiffert
International Security Affairs
Department of Defense

George Moose
Bureau of African Affairs
Department of State

William K. Parmenter
National Intelligence Officer for Africa
Central Intelligence Agency

Robert I. Rotberg
Massachusetts Institute of Technology

Michael A. Samuels
Center for Strategic and International Studies

Dimitri K. Simes
Center for Strategic and International Studies

Helmut Sonnenfeldt
Brookings Institution

W. Scott Thompson
Tufts University

Thomas Thornton
National Security Council

Jiri Valenta
Naval Postgraduate School

Dunstan Wai
The Rockefeller Foundation

Thomas W. Wolfe
Rand Corporation

Donald S. Zagoria
Research Institute on Social Change
Columbia University

I. William Zartman
New York University

About the authors . . . . .

Michael A. Samuels is Executive Director for Third World Studies of the Center for Strategic and International Studies of Georgetown University. From 1975 to 1977 he served as U.S. Ambassador to the Republic of Sierra Leone.

Dr. Samuels, who holds a Ph.D. in African History from Columbia University, has published several books and articles on African, Portuguese, and trade subjects: *Portuguese Africa – A Handbook* (Praeger, 1969), co–authored; *History of Education in Angola, 1878 to 1914* (Teacher's College Press, 1970); and "The Nigeria–Biafra Conflict" (CSIS, 1970), editor; as well as several articles on southern Africa, Angola, Portugal, and U.S. trade problems. In 1978 he edited a special White Paper on The Horn of Africa that served as a supplement to *The Washington Review of Strategic and International Studies* and has authored reports on a number of countries in Africa.

Chester A. Crocker is the Director of African Studies at CSIS and Associate Professor of International Relations, Georgetown University. Dr. Crocker received his Ph.D. from the Johns Hopkins School of Advanced International Studies, after which he served as news editor of *Africa Report*. In 1970 he joined the National Security Council as a Staff Officer. From 1972–1978 he was Director of Georgetown University's Master of Science in Foreign Service Program. Dr. Crocker is the author of many articles and monographs, including the recently published, *From Rhodesia to Zimbabwe: The Fine Art of Transition* (1977) and *Namibia at the Crossroads: Economic and Political Prospects* (1978, with Dr. Penelope Hartland–Thunberg), both CSIS monographs. He is co–editor of *South Africa into the 1980s* (1979) and has completed field research on a forthcoming study of South Africa's evolving relationship with the Western nations.

Roger W. Fontaine is Director of Latin American Studies at CSIS. He received his M.A. and Ph.D. from the Johns Hopkins School of Advanced International Studies. Dr. Fontaine's most recent publications include *Latin America: Struggle for Progress*, and a book for the Praeger Special Studies,

Latin America's New Internationalism. He is also the author of a CSIS *Washington Paper* on *The Andean Pact: A Political Analysis* (1977) and has written numerous articles in major American newspapers.

* **Dimitri K. Simes** is Director of Soviet Studies at CSIS and also serves as coordinator for the Congressional Luncheon Seminar and Senior Congressional Staff Conference series on national security issues. Since joining CSIS in 1973, Dr. Simes has authored many studies relative to his research on the Soviet political leadership, aspects of Soviet foreign and domestic policy, and U.S.–Soviet relations. The most recent of these include *Soviet Succession: Leadership in Transition* (1978) and *Détente and Conflict: Soviet Foreign Policy 1972–1977* (1977). His articles and commentaries have appeared in *Foreign Policy*, The *Proceedings of the Academy of Political Science*, and *The Journal of International Affairs*, as well as *The New York Times, Time*, The *Washington Star*, and *Newsweek*. Dr. Simes attended Moscow State University and a graduate school of the Institute of World Economy and International Relations of the USSR Academy of Sciences, where he was a Research Associate from 1967 to 1972.

Robert E. Henderson, Research Associate in Third World Studies at CSIS, is a 1972 graduate of Harvard College and has completed work in the Master of Science in Foreign Service program of Georgetown University, focusing on North/South security issues with an African specialization. He was a member of the Freedom House Observer Mission to Zimbabwe in April, 1979, and has written several articles on African political and security issues.

LIBRARY OF DAVIDSON COLLEGE

Books on regular loan may be checked out for **two weeks**. Books must be presented at the Circulation Desk in order to be renewed.

A fine is charged after date due.

Special books are subject to special regulations at the discretion of the library staff.